Being Present
A Guide to Connecting

Casey K. McEwen

1 - WHAT QUALIFIES ME TO WRITE THIS BOOK?

I ALWAYS ASK WHY. I was born with an intense curiosity, natural insecurity, ego the size of _____ (fill in your favorite large land mass) and an awareness that I can only describe as a gift and a curse. After I was caught bragging at an early age regarding my ability to memorize, I was told "the puppet memorizes facts to repeat while the wise man asks 'why' and gains wisdom". Sounded like a bunch of hooey back then and I couldn't have cared less but of course, I never forgot. Later the simple truth presented itself to me like a baseball bat alongside the head in a professional setting and when I reflected, the message came back fast and hard. I learned.

So, I like to ask Why and understand Why. I am a student of people. In fact, I would give myself an "A+". Beyond experiences of primary and secondary research, focus groups and traditional mediums of analysis, I most like to glean the insights that are personal and actionable. The ones that are important because they make a difference.

You find them everywhere if you look, and I have looked. In the classroom, the park bench, the board room, the bathroom, the mall, local sporting events, the hospital, the casino, the church pew, the grocery store, the soup line, the gas station, the job line, in celebrations, funeral homes, school yards, the VFW, the coffee shop (Starbucks of course) and the list goes on and on.

The people watching is good, but the people insights are fantastic!

Another part of my qualification AND credibility is that I fail every day. I've made more mistakes than almost everyone I know. I've taught myself to call those mistakes "experiments" and count them as one less viable option as I press forward to a solution. I plant the seeds of each one of them in all my relationships and endeavors. I've been aware enough and curious enough to learn from my mistakes AND those around me and, I ALWAYS ASK WHY.

2 - INTRODUCTION

The Objective of This Book

This book has a simple objective. It is to illustrate the value in *Being Present* and to help you move in that direction because you believe in the value.

The Quotes

You will see quotes sprinkled throughout this book from many people far smarter than I am with opinions and perspectives that I think are in some way relevant to the message of *Being Present*. Some will be familiar, and others will make you think. I hope some of them inspire you, some of them haunt you, some of them stick with you and some of them you repeat to your friends and family.

The Takeaways

At the end of each Chapter there is a list of Takeaways, which are meant to be the things you should consider actionable steps for you. I hope you make this your "short list" of things you are willing to try. Jot them on an index card or a note in your phone or the smallest of tattoos.

The Apology

Apologies in advance to those who are looking for the next big concept or idea. This won't be it. I'm sure you will not read anything here that is brilliant or even something that you didn't already know. My hope for you is only that you look at what you already DO KNOW differently and act on it.

The Change In You

Being Present is a simple concept. Simple to understand and therefore easy to dismiss. But for those who see it for what it is – a way to truly connect better with the people most important to you and the way to dramatically improve individual performance – your life will be changed forever for the better. (wow that was a long sentence)

The Dedication

I dedicate this book to my wife Grady and wonderful children Logan, Jessica, Mackenzie and Austin and the many friends I'm blessed to have.

3 - WHAT YOU WILL LEARN

The name of this book is **Being Present** and subtitled "A Guide to Connecting". The truth is that the objective of this book is to teach you how to "connect" and **Being Present** is simply the best way to do that.

When you consider connecting better with those you care about or even having richer engagements with anyone, you will be challenged in this book to think about the reason WHY. Why at your core do you want to connect better? Think about that. Why is it important? What's the value in it? Why do it at all? I would submit it is because you WANT to be better, you hope that you CAN be better, and you want to learn HOW.

This book explores the challenges we face connecting to others in our personal, business, friends and family relationships. It explains the enriching but intrusive nature of Social Media and its impact on our lives and how to effectively manage it.

You will learn how to put down your phone and be in the moment (being present) with the person in front of you.

This book explains the many values of being present and also the relationship devastation, monetary impact and even life-threatening dangers of not being present.

You will understand how to explore and change the family culture you have created or allowed to happen inside your home. You will learn exactly how to change that family culture for the better.

As an employee you will learn how being present at work can make you happier, healthier and wealthier and give you a permanent competitive edge. You will learn how using these concepts will make a huge difference in your career trajectory.

As an employer or manager or leader or business owner you will learn how you can grow top performers by incorporating a focus on being present into the environmental programming of your organizational structure and your culture.

You will learn WHO is actually most important to be present with and why. This will change your behavior with that audience forever more.

You will learn how to use meditating, affirmations, iconology, acronyms, advanced sales techniques and other ways to train yourself to be better at being present. These techniques will double and triple your personal effectiveness.

In this book you will get actionable takeaways and real solutions for modifying your own behavior so that you can capture the most from those relationships that hold the most value to you.

By the end, you will understand through the many examples given that the greatest gift you can give another person is being present AND you will know exactly how to do that.

4 - THE MEANING OF "BEING PRESENT" AND MY STORY

OK – So let's get started! Being Present is a relatively simple concept as you are about to see. Here are a couple of examples that we will go into much greater detail about later in the book.

The Definition:
I believe the best definition of **_Being Present_** is to be singularly focused on the person or task at hand.

Being Present means to that you have the opportunity to give the greatest gift you can give another human being – your COMPLETE attention. There is NO better way to connect with others.

Being Present means giving your complete and undivided attention to the person or task before you. It means making a conscious effort to remove all mental and physical distractions so that you can apply the BEST of your talents and be in that moment.

Being Present means having the personal discipline to NOT immediately respond to the phone text or social media notification, the door opening, the song playing, the nagging sensation that you are forgetting something. It means being proactive in your self-management posture to REDUCE distractions.

Being Present means choosing this time, this moment, this person or task and elevating it to be the most important thing to you. You have honored this person or made this task most important by elevating it NOW and giving it this high level of attention.

Being Present means that you choose to engage at **your best** level. You are choosing to give that present interaction or activity the best that is within you.

Do you want to be better? Read on.

You might wonder how this subject is worthy of a book. My answer is that it's worthy of many books by people who are better than I am at communicating the value of this concept. I will share with you that I came across the concept in a different way.

You see YOU have already been exposed to the concept of being present just like I have many times before in your life. But probably like me, you heard it these ways: "Hey son, pay attention! Don't you see what you are doing?"
"You have to focus on this if you want to be better."
"Stop spacing out and listen to me."
"Keep your head up or you're going to get hit by a bus one of these days!"

I mean come on - even at the drawing for the county fundraiser you "must be present to win".

Don't these sound familiar? They should. These are only a few of the many ways we have all heard from our parents that we need to Be Present. Now they probably didn't say those exact words, but the meaning was clear. Pay attention or bad stuff will happen!

My Story

My story about how I realized the value in being present and eventually why I wanted to write this book was simply around me being observant (one of the very few things I do well) and then a moment of self-awareness when I became VERY embarrassed.

I was at a neighborhood cookout. You know the kind. Saturday afternoon, great weather, ten families, seventy or so kids, lots of libations, etc. I was considered senior management at work at the time and had just finished a seminar about the practical applications of "listening versus hearing". I'm not sure how much I actually listened to (ha ha) but some of it must have stuck.

So eventually the guys gather to an area where we talk about and lie about everything. We assign a wife lookout whose job it is to be the signaler in the event of a possible spousal unit overhearing us and now it's GAME ON. Everything was on-track and normal except that one of our party participants was recently unemployed and concerned about his situation. He was legitimately worried about finances and his family and was hoping to share his situation and get feedback, suggestions, leads, advice... anything from our neighborhood group! I actually "listened" and was very sympathetic to his situation. What I also noticed was that there was probably only one other guy who did the same thing. Two out of ten? The rest were barely engaged between looking at phones, side jokes, yelling at kids, drink refills, etc. It was sad.

The truth is I was really NO better than they were. I had just had some carryover from the listening versus hearing seminar. Now you might think we were just a bunch of jerks. OK - probably true but I think we'd all like to believe we'd be more supportive and engaged than the example I just gave. But during the cookout I saw my same friends ignore their kids or give them distracted answers to important questions like "Dad, can me and Donny and Mike throw the ninja stars at the girls?" Distracted Dad – "Sure – just be careful." Or the ignoring of the wife who reminded Dad multiple times that they had another commitment with family the same night which was also ignored – multiple times. Or the wife who asks her husband if it's OK for the chicken on the grill to be "a little pink". I don't know how or why it clicked with me in that moment, but it did. It was also when I was sure I HAD ALSO FAILED! I knew that was ME probably hundreds or maybe even thousands of times before. I had a bunch of little flashbacks in my mind of times when I had given the easy, distracted answer.

Times when something small but bad happened. Times when one of my kids had said "But you said I could Dad..." (insert skinned knee) or "But you said you'd take me there..." (I already committed somewhere else) or "I told you that two days ago on the phone" (I was mentally absent) and a lot of other relationship examples. I wondered how many times I was one of the eight other guys who didn't engage with a friend in need. I felt some shame in intuitively knowing it had probably been a lot of times.

Well this revelation did not make me do a personal 180-degree turn around and instantly be the best at *being present*. It simply started me on a path. I didn't know what I wanted to be, but I DID know what I didn't want to be. My future from that point will likely be similar to yours after reading this book. It started slow. I began to be aware of situations where others and myself were not being present. I also began to put pieces together of my past stories where the result might have been different if I had been present. From conversations to car accidents they were many. Overall, I felt lucky that nothing worse had happened in most cases and shame for all the times my selfishness caused pain or hurt feelings.

After a very short while I was amazed at how many times a day, I would observe strangers, friends, neighbors, colleagues and family members not being present. It was staggering and I had NO idea what to do with the knowledge. I failed 20-30 times a day and I KNEW what to look out for! Just changing my personal habits was really tough. But I was committed because I had now seen the many impacts of not ***being present***. Then I was hearing about everything from life and death distracted driving stories to relationship ending events with devastating impacts to families. Work stories and personal relationship stories and family stories. And still – what was I supposed to do with this? I started by wanting to help but not knowing how. All I did was notice stuff, write down stuff and occasionally say stuff. Then as people began to know I had a point of view on this subject they would tell me stories that reinforced the value in ***being present***. They might be stories of failures or stories that affirmed better and different ways to be present. Eventually I felt a compelled to share this concept with a wider audience in the hope that it could do one or both of two things.

1. It could make someone think twice about the physical, emotional and relationship dangers of NOT being present.
2. It could communicate the appeal of the interpersonal value of being present and change lives for the better.

My Solution: Become a relationship evangelist for this simple needed change in our everyday lives. It started with individual conversations, led to groups and now to this book.

I hope you will also see and use the value in ***being present***!

Quote:

"The secret of health for both mind and body is not to mourn for the past, worry about the future, or anticipate troubles, but to live in the present moment wisely and earnestly." - Buddha

5 - THE GREATEST GIFT

The greatest gift you can give someone is your complete attention. There is nothing better or more powerful or impactful. It truly is, the greatest gift.

Some people are actually known for the personal trait of *being present*. One example that might be familiar with many who read this because he is known universally is Bill Clinton (politics aside). It is said that no matter who you are from Head of State to public utility worker to farmer, if you are having a conversation with him, you KNOW there is nothing more important to him at that moment than that conversation. He is completely engaged. You feel as though he TRULY respects and values your opinion and the time, he has with you. There are many others who have been described similarly. Who do you know personally that you would describe that way? Is there ANYONE you would describe that way in your life?

"He was always completely engaged, respectful of your opinion and giving of attention." Now isn't that what we would ALL like said about us? Can you imagine a better compliment?

Can you imagine how it feels to be the person receiving that attention? How it feels to know, to KNOW, **TO KNOW** that there is nothing more important in the world at this moment to the person in front of me than what I have to say. They are truly engaged with me. All the body language and perceptible cues are on point because it is truly sincere.

For me as the receiver, I feel... I feel... appreciated, validated that what I'm sharing is of worth, and good because that person was right here in this moment with me. They aren't looking at their phone or their watch or anyone else. I have their complete attention and it makes me feel good about me and it makes me feel good about them. It's a fantastic feeling and an incredible gift to receive and/or that you can give someone.

So, let me ask you again, who do you know that you would describe as someone who makes you feel that way? Do you know of one? Is there anyone in your life who left you with that impression? Parent? Pastor? Neighbor? Friend? The person you love most?

Have you even ever met anyone who made you think they could possibly be that kind of person? If not, maybe YOU are the one who is supposed to carry the torch and be that person for others. Maybe YOU will be the difference in others' lives through your changed behavior. Maybe YOU were meant to be a giver of the greatest gift!

A Kid Example

A good friend of mine, Morgan Hill, who is a much better author than I am (look him up) was CEO of a company we both worked for years ago.

One day he came by for dinner and my youngest son Austin (three at the time) decided it was lap time. "Uncle Morgan" picked him up and we continued to talk. Austin loved Morgan and wanted to babble at him – which he did but Morgan continued to talk to me. Four or five times during the conversation, Austin would grab Morgan's face with both of his little hands and turn his face toward him so he could look at him and babble directly at him. He wanted his complete attention and finally he got it because WE finally "got it". That complete attention is all any of us want and at three years old, some of us are bold enough to grab someone by the face to get it!

That story has been retold many times over the years by Morgan through his ministry work and by me. Both of us knowing it was a precious and pure moment of truth. The greatest gift you can give anyone, and especially a child, is your complete attention.

Takeaways:

- Try to be the giver of the greatest gift because it truly is what everyone on the planet wants. The only feeling better than being the receiver is to be the giver of "The Greatest Gift". Once you've done it – you'll be sold!
- If you don't know anyone who has developed this gift among all of your friends and family, maybe, just maybe it is "supposed to be you".
- Sometimes you just have to grab someone by the face and babble directly at them!

Quote:

"Living in the moment means letting go of the past and not waiting for the future. It means living your life consciously, aware that each moment you breathe is a gift." -- Oprah Winfrey

6 - BEING MORE PRESENT

In order to be MORE Present, you have to understand how present you currently are. You have to understand how you spend your time and decide that YOU CONTROL it and that YOU CAN modify it. Then you can be MORE Present.

How do I spend my mental time?

Think of it like a pie chart and know that you spend time constantly cycling in differing percentages but only in three buckets: Past, Present and Future

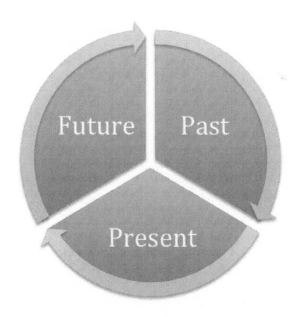

The Past - We all spend mental time in the past. We relive the great times we've enjoyed. We treasure those times when we felt so good about who we were in those moments. We all love to relive those memories of our happiest times when "we won" at something or with someone. Then some of us hold onto grudges and pain (<— get some help with that), some of us replay situations and events and torment ourselves about what we could have done differently. We play the mental tapes of "If only I had done this, or said this, things today might be different." We beat ourselves up with the "what might have beens". Some of us love to remember those times when we had that great personal relationship with a loved one or friend. Or that awesome recognition for a job well done at work. Or maybe it's just that picture of you in bell-bottom jeans and a mullet holding that big fish.

We all spend mental time in the past and some of that time is productive and some isn't. If your objective reflections help you to not repeat mistakes or improve outcomes, then that time is well spent. But how much of your day or week is spent in that Past bucket? Do you have any idea? Probably not and that's OK for now.

The Future - We all spend some time hoping and dreaming. We spend time planning, we spend time setting goals and visualizing what we want our lives to look like whether that's next week, next month or in years to come. There's nothing wrong with visualizing what you want as the first step in actualizing your goals. It's a healthy and smart move. But we also spend time worrying about people or things we don't control and that can consume us and ruin our "present". If you are honest, you will agree that this is you (and all of us) sometimes. Some of us spend our mental time about the future differently based on if it's work related versus personal and relationship related. Some of us are planners for as much as we can in our personal and professional lives and spend a great deal of time mapping out "the plan" with contingencies and "Plan B's and C's". Again, some of that time is spent well and some isn't. How much time of your day or week is spent in the Future bucket?

The Present - The mental time you spend in the Past AND Future is time you are not *Being Present*.

You can't stop yourself from thinking about the Past or Future and you shouldn't. There is definite value in analyzing the past to learn from it and looking forward to plan and actualize your dreams. What you can ALSO do is to make a conscious effort to focus more on the Present. It's here and now and you're armed with your cumulative experience and judgment to help you not repeat mistakes and to make this your best chance at making your future a reality. It's in focusing on the things you do NOW, in this moment, that make your tomorrow.

The way you choose to spend your Present will ultimately be the deciding factor in your level of happiness and fulfillment.

Make no mistake, it is a choice – YOUR choice. It's a choice that you can condition into a repeatable habit that will enrich your life beyond your wildest dreams.

Q: When it comes to trying to be More Present, how much failure is acceptable or normal along the way?

A: However much it takes!

The REAL Truth is that there is NO failure when you are moving forward to be **more present**. There are only varying degrees of success. The moment you decide you are going to improve, you have. You may not execute all of the interactions the way you wanted but you've already begun to effect a positive personal change.

It's a journey and ANY improvement are good. You and those you care about will benefit. You literally cannot fail!

One of the challenges is to spend the appropriate time in the Past and Future mental buckets. So, what is "appropriate"? Who knows? I'm sure it is situational, but I doubt there is an answer that is 100% definitive and correct. The closest I think we can come to an answer is to know that we want to maximize the amount of time we spend in **The Present** bucket. Part of that process means we would reduce the amount of unproductive time we spend in the other buckets.

The best way to begin is to spend ONE day tracking and recording how you spend your time as a benchmark. Please let me stress that this is a one-time activity that you should not have to repeat to gain the learnings from it. If you find you are really out of whack, then you may want to repeat the process farther down the road to see what progress you've made.

Takeaways:

- Determine how you currently spend your mental time.
- YOU control how you spend your mental time so YOU can adjust to spend more time in the present bucket.
- Choose to create a habit of ***Being Present***.
- Any improvement is a win for you and those you care about.

Quote:

> *"What we are today comes from our thoughts of yesterday, and our present thoughts build our life of tomorrow: Our life is the creation of our mind."* – Buddha

7 - WHY ARE YOU READING THIS BOOK?

So why are you reading this book? Which one are you?

I'm a Victim of my companies' executive book of the month club selection and I couldn't care less about this book. Please Please Please – just let me get to the end of this painful train wreck of a book so I can get back to my Facebook feed and a Martini and then maybe some good red wine.

Someone Gave It To Me – Not a good answer but good you at least got to this page. The strafing run mini-intervention Dr. Phil (no offense intended to the good Doctor) sound bite advice of "you got a problem – here – read this book" rarely sits well with most folks. I get that. I hope you will actually give it a chance and find something here that resonates with you and that you can use.

I Want to Be Better – Ding Ding Ding – We have a winner! For whatever reason you are ready to invest in YOU. That normally means you receive the information with a more open mind than if it were pushed on you. You will get more out of this than a thousand others who are forced to read it. (Big assumption here is that a thousand people will read this book.)

At some point in their lives, most people get to a place where they say to themselves "I want to be a better me". The reason WHY they are in that place determines how seriously their intent and commitment will be to actually being better. If this is where you are, I'm happy for you and happier still that you may get something here that you see value in.

I think you will find that just being open to the opportunity to be better will let you get more out of the concept of ***being present***. As often as you can recognize yourself and your habits and your perspective on certain subjects, the more likely you will make some gains from this book.

Takeaway:

It doesn't matter how you got here – you ARE here. I promise you; this will be worth your time.
Be open and look for examples of YOU. If you see yourself, you can make positive changes.

Quote:

"One today is worth two tomorrows." -- Benjamin Franklin

8 - CAN YOU SEE ME? OR YOU?

Do any of these situations sound like what you sometimes experience?

Can you drive to work or home or to any particular well-known destination and all of the sudden arrive there and not really know how you made it there? You probably can't remember anything specific between the two places, only that you arrived. Guess what - your brain was somewhere else!

Do you ever "spaz" while in traffic and come back to the present by the sound of the car horn behind you?

Have you heard from your spouse or kids, "well - I told you that" and you don't even remember the conversation? You were probably part of that conversation, but you obviously weren't engaged.

Have you been at the dinner table in the middle of full-blown family dinner and conversation and think "I really need to make sure I address blah-blah-blah with blah-blah-blah". Your focus wavers and next thing you know, your spousal unit is screaming "Did you hear what I said?" (insert "No" here)

Have you been at work in a meeting and not paying attention because you're thinking about something at home OR the same thing happens when you're on the phone OR (it gets even worse – wait for it,... wait for it,...) the same thing happens FACE to FACE in the middle of a conversation?

Or how about this one since I hear it most often:

When I'm at work I'm at home and when I'm at home I'm at work.

When I'm at work I'm of course focused on the work tasks I am responsible to complete and because I give it my all, I spend a lot of time at work. When I'm there and because I spend so much time there, I feel GUILTY about not being at home and not doing the things at home that I probably should have done. I should have done _____ around the house. I should have said _____ to my spouse. I really should have made time to do _____ with one of my kids. I really needed to call my friend back and say _____. I should have fixed that one thing around the house that I've been meaning to do forever. Which leads to even more random - I wonder if the proof of insurance cards in our cars are current. My focus wavers and the next thing I know I've lost some important time, or I wasn't paying attention to something I should have and.... (insert bad consequence here).

Sound familiar? Does this look or sound like you? If so, how OFTEN does this sound or look like you? Is this you some of the time? Is this you most of the time or maybe you can't even remember a time when you didn't feel this way? If you never feel this way you should immediately throw this book in the trash and go back and sit on your throne of lies.

Now when I'm at home, it's exactly the opposite and I'm thinking about the things I still have to do at work. Oh, I forgot to send that email to _____. I need to make sure I call _____ tomorrow. I remember that I have that meeting at 2:00. What am I going to wear? I could make a much longer work list here but I'm sure you get the concept. I am supposed to be present and engaged with my family but clearly, I'm not!

Question: How do I reconcile this? How can I stop this internal process or habit of mental "Switching"?

Answer: Start by understanding more about the habit so you can begin to change it.

Be Aware - Ask Yourself Why - When you find yourself mentally changing direction or being distracted, ask yourself – why?
What is the distraction?
Is it something that is unresolved? Where does it "belong" meaning where does that thing belong in my life?

Write it Down - Writing it down gives you the power of knowing it's not going away. You won't forget it and even if you do, you will see it later and can react to it then. It's empowering to know that you have still in some small way – managed it.

Own It - Knowing that you haven't been able to manage all the little things that you have to juggle in your life on a daily basis is a constant drain on your attention. It drags you down. As soon as you understand that you will naturally try to avoid that. Conversely, knowing that you've dealt with or managed to put things in their proper boxes is gratifying. It's gratifying even if you haven't resolved them.

Takeaways:

* Everyone gets distracted and end up on auto-pilot sometimes. It doesn't have to be how you are most of the time.

- Most people think about work when they're home and vice versa. It's normal and with some training and focus you can reduce it dramatically.
- Ask yourself why you switch and try to write it down. Catch yourself in the act and be honest about the reason why.
- Acknowledge that you do it and you will naturally try to avoid doing it as well as manage it better.

Quote:

"Being in the moment involves giving maximum appreciation and love to your present experience." - Sara Paddison

9 - SWITCHING

What exactly is "Switching"?

There are two types of things commonly referred to as switching.
One is related to multi-tasking, which we will discuss later. The other
type of switching is the habit of mentally switching back and forth
between a present interaction or task and a distraction. The best
example is from the previous chapter of mentally... "When I'm at
work I'm at home and when I'm home, I'm at work."

Switching is different than your adult ADD, pre-frontal cortex-
hurting friend that you lose early in a conversation because they saw
something shiny. They need help! This is different. This happens
literally hundreds of times a day to millions of people.

If I Switch, does that mean there is something wrong with me?

Not at all. You are soooooooooooo normal.

I've had people say, "Oh please tell me you aren't introducing yet
another reason why we all can't be normal." I'm not. In fact, I believe
it's become more the norm as the task list in our ever increasingly
busy lives grows even larger. We are all juggling more balls and are
mentally tugged in more directions than ever before.

Who Switches?

Everyone.

I've been asked if there is a correlation between IQ and Switching.
The answer is a resounding NO. Everyone from Triple Nine Society

members to the banjo boy from Deliverance falls victim to the same bad habits. There is no person with a specific characterization, IQ, EQ, personality type, job type, family unit, etc. that is immune. It's just something that most of us do unconsciously.

The truth is you have a big awesome brain that can juggle a tremendous amount of complex information that we don't give it credit for. Your brain is like a computer than can receive and process information at an incredibly high speed.

What are the triggers for Switching?

There can be many triggers for switching but my research indicates they fall into two basic groups both of which can be managed to reduce the negative effects and help you *Be Present*.

The "Constant Group" is mostly comprised of the things that nag at your brain every day you breathe. They are the ones that creep into your head and distract you from what you should be doing at that moment. They are always just beneath the surface waiting to pop up and say "Hi – I can see you are doing something important so why don't we rehash this notion we can't resolve for a few." Yeah – That's fun isn't it? Next thing you know – you've lost time and probably momentum heading off in a mentally useless direction.

Guilt for the unaccomplished or unfulfilled can be a constant and because it is largely unresolved on a daily basis. Needed relationship repairs because of some past issues can just sit there and simmer in the back of your consciousness and distract you slightly every day. It's a drain on your ability to focus and *Be Present*.

These things seem small, but they build on each other and eventually become bigger than they really are. These make that Constant Group of distractions a mental snowball rolling down a hill getting bigger all the time.

The "Variable Group" is full of the artificial stimuli we ALLOW or INVITE into our lives and lifestyles. Examples are instant messaging, text messages, e-mails, social media notifications, email lists we subscribe to, friends we text, etc. These are actually easier to control or manage IF you are convinced to see the need to do so.

Part of the intent here is to help you realize that the switching happens and that you do have control over many of the ways to manage it.

Takeaways:

- Try to be conscious of switching when it happens. Just by doing that one thing you will have an impact and slowly be able to change the habit.
- Be aware of what falls in your "constant group" versus your variable group".
- Choose what you ALLOW or INVITE carefully. Give it some real thought.

Quote:

"In rivers, the water that you touch is the last of what has passed and the first of that which comes; so with present time." - Leonardo da Vinci

10 - FACEBOOK IS THE DEVIL

Facebook is the Devil – OK, OK not really. I'm actually a Facebook fan but an unmanaged use of it and other Social Media promotes behavior that amplifies the interpersonal gap in *being present*.

Will Facebook change in this way? I believe no or if so, only for the better but be prepared for the "Social Media me too's" that are already in play and still to come. There are already hundreds of variations on the theme. Personally, I loves me some Instagram, Snapchat, Marco Polo, LinkedIn and I confess losing a complete weekend building my boards on Pinterest. (don't judge me)

Social media is here to stay, and I believe that's a good thing. The question becomes "how do I deal with it"? How do WE deal with it? What we have to navigate as a society (and a global one at that) is how, if at all, we allow Social Media to change the way we interact at the **most important levels**.

The answer is that we **don't allow it** to change how, or interfere with, the fundamental way we connect with each other.

There is a dynamic to Social Media that enriches our lives, but it ALSO requires a level of attentiveness to the medium that reduces our ability to **be present** (unless we manage it).

Those who engage in social media at a high level not only are the high volume "posters", but they also wear their sense of urgency or immediacy to respond like a badge. They are the First Responders of the Ethernet. First to "Like", first to comment and like the movie series, they are Fast and Furious. "Look at me, Look at me and what I did!"

"Like"ing something has replaced the need to communicate. To say congratulations on the phone or face to face or to send an email or to actually send REAL mail.

"Like"ing something is telling the poster that you saw what they did and you publicly approve/thought was funny/thought it was sad/agrees with the point of view, also love crazy cat video's, etc.

What most folks won't admit to is that it is also saying "I'm here" remember me? I liked yours so I hope you will LIKE mine. It's the newest coolest game sweeping the world and it's called "Quid Pro Like". That's sarcasm kids!

It is "relationship abbreviating" and it's the same when you are "favoriting tweets" or many other examples in various forms in social media environments. It is NOT engaging in a real or meaningful way. Should you stop doing it? I'm not suggesting that. I do it too but please just understand what it is and don't let it replace the opportunity to connect when you can and to *Be Present* when you can.

I have a friend that told me when she realized the truth in the example of relationship abbreviating, she changed her approach a little. She still "likes" lots of things in Facebook and Instagram but now she takes the extra time to add what she hopes is a meaningful comment. She says she "likes" a lot less in volume but thinks she sees more value in her current practice than before. You know what? I kinda "like" that.

So again – Social Media is not bad. It's good and life enriching but you have to manage it if you want to *Be Present*.

"You can be anyone in your digital life, but you can only be the BEST of YOU when you're present in your real life." <— Hey...Why don't you post that? I promise to "like" it!

REMEMBER – None of the best moments of your life will happen while you are looking at a screen.

Managing Social Media helps you to Be Present.

Finding a way to manage the social media venues you are engaged in will help you **be present**. You will find that you don't actually miss anything, you just schedule when you receive it versus it being a 24/7-shotgun blast of digital yadda-yadda- yadda, blah-blah-blah.

Opting Out - You will probably find that you will want to "Opt Out" on some things that you really don't see high value in and on others be very, very selective. This help more than you can imagine.

Notification Management - Use the options provided within each social media forum, email subscription and your device to manage what notifications you receive and how often you receive them.

I've seen in family or group settings people who create the "no phone zone". No phones at the dinner table whether it's at home or in a restaurant. No phones in meetings.

We've probably all been out to eat somewhere and seen the family of four at the next table with all of their heads buried in their phones including Mom and Dad. No conversation, no interaction, no sharing, no connecting. No one was *Being Present*.

Recently saw this one and it crushed me. Picture a Dad and five-year-old daughter at dinner on a Saturday night. I happened to know him, but I was sitting a few tables away. This was a visitation weekend dinner with his daughter Amanda. Dad's head was buried in his phone the entire time before the meal and even during the meal. Amanda tried talking to him at least 9 times before the food came.

He gave her short, quick replies, no eye contact and seemed impatient. How would you guess Amanda felt? What would you guess is the only thing she wanted in the world during that time with her Dad? A slice of that time-pie? Just a sliver of Dad attention on her plate would have gone a long way. How easy would it have been for him to give her the most important thing in her world at that moment?

Soooooo is Dad a jerk? Well he kind of is but that's another story. Dad didn't see or realize how important that interaction was. Maybe he thought what he was doing was more important. IF he knew, would he have reacted differently? Maybe. If he valued the relationship with his daughter, then probably yes.

The ONLY reason I'm not including his real name is that I'm going to send him this book. (but it rhymes with weave and starts with an "St")

Takeaways:

• Social Media is life enriching when managed. Don't let it interfere in how you connect with others. Don't be a relationship abbreviator.

• Review your current long list of Social Media and Emails and Opt OUT of the ones that don't really add value.

- Adjust the notifications on your phone to reduce the distractions. This makes an immediate difference.

- Don't be a Steve.

Quote:

Every morning is a fresh beginning. Every day is the world made new. Today is a new day. Today is my world made new. I have lived all my life up to this moment, to come to this day. This moment--this day--is as good as any moment in all eternity. I shall make of this day--each moment of this day--a heaven on earth. This is my day of opportunity.

-- Dan Custer

11 - WHAT'S THE BIG DEAL?

I mean really - is **Being Present** a big deal? One interesting
perspective to have on this or other issues when they come up is
"How relevant is this issue to me and my life?"

One of the ways I use (and suggest you try) to litmus test relevancy
and whether I'm going off on a tangent versus addressing something
of real substance is to ask a question. Is this new or a fad or is just
another "this too shall pass" moment? Was this a problem 25 years
ago or will it still be 25 years from now?

So, when YOU decide if **Being Present** is a big deal or not, I'd
suggest you consider these additional questions:

Who's complaining about it (not being present)? I think more
and more people every day. You will hear it if you listen. It's easy to
hear in the family setting. Whether it's parents talking to distracted
kids or kids talking to distracted parents, it's evident and heard in our
homes. The same is true in the workplace. It's the reason behind
policy changes related to meetings (no cell phones, no laptops) and
many other examples. From Safety Captains to HR Managers to
anyone just trying to get something done with other people, you will
hear the complaints.

Do I even really notice it (not being present)? I think many of us
didn't really notice it in the past, but it was still an issue. Today more
people are picking up on the issue and the social cues attached to it.
Once you see it, you will ALWAYS see it. Today you really do notice
when people aren't engaged with you or others. The truth is you've
always known it even if you didn't know what to call the behavior.

**Does anyone else I know think it's a problem (not being
present)?** If you are like me and my friends and family, it's a BIG

yes! This is probably a big yes for you also. We all have examples we can cite, and we all recognize that the issue is getting harder to deal with and not easier. In fact, "dealing with distraction" whether you are the communicator or the communicatee is one of our biggest interpersonal challenges today.

Is not being present affecting me? Here the answer is yes simply by virtue of your knowledge of the issue. You now recognize it and therefore you give it credibility in your mind. You don't like it when you see that someone is not being present with you. That certainly affects you if you are trying to communicate something that you see value in. It also changes the way you view that person. Whether you previously held them in high or esteem doesn't matter. You will view them differently going forward and perhaps consciously or unconsciously like them less.

Is it affecting my relationships (not being present)? Well of course silly rabbit! Every day in so many ways it IS affecting you. Whether it's a personal or professional relationship you "Must be Present to Win". If you are the one not **being present,** then you are missing out and so is the other person in that relationship. If the other person is the one not **being present,** then they are missing out, but you are also. You are not getting or giving all that could be a benefit. Either way – it's affecting you and not in a positive way.

Are things really different now? Whether you are comparing the number or types of distractions to what was present 25 years ago the answer is a resounding YES. Did we have interpersonal distractions 25 or 50 years ago? Of course we did but they were not as prevailing or as intrusive as today. They were not as large a part of our culture as they are today. There were not as many opportunities for distraction through visual, verbal and social means. And now we have social media as a large influence in all of our lives. Things really ARE different now.

So is it really a big deal?

What do you think?

After all - what's the downside to NOT *Being Present*? .

..

...

....

.....

12 - A SAD STORY OF NOT BEING PRESENT

In the 90's, I was working for a truly great company. We were a diverse group of multi-unit management who were highly trained, ambitious professionals and there was nothing we could not do or load we could not carry.

One of the ways we grew so well was that we were rewarded when we added people to the team who were "as good as or better" than we were. It made a difference. I had one of those guys on my team rising quickly through the ranks and had success written all over him. Sharp personable guy, great communicator, wonderful wife, and beautiful young kids – you know the kind of guy.

One weekend day while at home he was working furiously on a work project with reports and papers scattered everywhere, making urgent calls and juggling a lot of balls. As his wife is leaving to run some errands, she tells him that she is taking the baby with her and he needs to watch their two-year-old. He absently shakes his head in acknowledgement and waves her off. A couple of hours later she returns to find him where she left him but their two-year-old floating dead in the hot tub.

It could have happened to anyone, but it didn't. I'm sure there are many other stories but this one I knew firsthand. It was a personal story that had devastating affects to them and their family and a story that leaves a lasting impression on everyone who hears it. Anything else I share as a disadvantage of not **Being Present** pales in comparison.

Takeaway:

The worst thing you can imagine CAN actually happen. You have a lot to lose in certain situations if you are not present.

Quote:

"Remember then: there is only one time that is important--Now! It is the most important time because it is the only time when we have any power." -- Leo Tolstoy

Still Not Convinced?

Not convinced there is a real disadvantage that could affect you or your family? Try looking up a YouTube video for an Anti-texting while driving PSA (Public Service Announcement). The danger message is the same as with drunk driving in that the offender doesn't ONLY kill themselves. The issue with texting while driving is that it still doesn't have the heightened negative awareness it should. The danger is socially understated while at the same time the number of deaths is on a dramatic rise.

Not Being Present in a Car

It's commonly referred to as "distracted driving" and though there are other reasons attributed to distracted driving, texting while driving is most dangerous. In fact, it has become such an American epidemic and insurance companies are suffering such great losses that they are now passing the cost of the losses to ALL of us! That's right ALL of us will pay more as a result of distracted drivers! Tick you off? It should. Here are some statistics that should scare you:

Texting While Driving Causes:

- 1,600,000 accidents per year – National Safety Council.
- 330,000 injuries per year – Harvard Center for Risk Analysis Study.
- 11 teen deaths EVERY DAY – Insurance Institute for Highway Safety Fatality Facts.
- Nearly 25% of ALL car accidents.

Texting While Driving is about 6 times more likely to cause an accident than driving intoxicated.

- The same as driving after 4 beers – National Highway Transportation Safety Admin.
- The number one driving distraction reported by teen drivers.

Texting While Driving:

- Makes you 23X more likely to crash – National Highway Transportation Safety Admin.
- Is the same as driving blind for 5 seconds at a time – VA. Tech Transportation Institute.
- Takes place by 800,000 drivers at any given time across the country.
- Slows your brake reaction speed by 18% – Human Factors & Ergonomics Society.
- Leads to a 400% increase with eyes off the road.

If someone is texting and driving, they are distracted and definitely not *Being Present.*

Still Still Still Not Convinced?

This will scare you because YOU have seen it.

Interview with Kidnapper/Sex Offender (we will call him Joe)

Q: How did you decide when or where to select a victim?
A: *Hell, that was the easiest part. You can go just about anywhere and catch a girl in the parking lot of the mall or Walmart or grocery. They don't look up. They never look up. They're always in their phones. They're not even talking to anyone – they're just texting. All I have to do is be between them and the door of the building. They made it easy.*

Q: Did you take them on the way in or on the way out?
A: *I always liked on the way out better. Then they're e still on their phones but they had one less hand cause they were carrying something else. They're too stupid to even pay attention.*

Trust me, you don't want to hear any more of that story.

Question: Are our daughters' easier targets because they are NOT present? Answer: ABSOLUTELY they are. What are YOU going to do about it Mom? Dad? Brother? Friend?

OK – on to an easier example.

How many of us have been annoyed by, almost hit, had to honk at "the teen texter" walking in or out of the same place we are going? If you are a driver you probably answered yes.

How many of us see the car swerving in the lane in front of us and when we pass them and look over see someone looking back and forth between their phone and the road? It happens all the time.

How many of us have missed our chance to get through that left turn light because someone's face was buried in his or her phone? ALL of us! I've recently started doing something I think is a public service that most of my friends think prove I'm a jerk. Unless I'm at the front of the turn lane, when the arrow shows up, I given my horn two gentle taps. Just a light roadrunner like "beep-beep". Just a little reminder to the turn lane population that it's time to pause the Facebook "Like"ing and do what we're here to do. Trust me that heads pop up and it actually works. Less road rage, faster commutes – everybody wins! Now I'm not advocating that everyone do this,... wait – actually I AM! Try it and be a socially responsible jerk like me!

Takeaways:

- NOT being present can have negative effects that range from irritating to fatal. Take it seriously and give it the importance it deserves. Ask yourself where you present risk to yourself or others in your daily life by not being present.
- Is it a real problem? YES
- Do we have a lot to lose? YES
- Are our daughters' easier targets because they are NOT present?

ABSOLUTELY they are. What are YOU going to do about it Mom? Dad? Brother? Friend?

Quote:

Yesterday is a canceled check; tomorrow is a promissory note; today is the only cash you have - so spend it wisely -- Kay Lyons

13 - WHAT DOES IT COST?

What does it cost when you're NOT present? There are a few ways to view this.

In personal situations– how many hundreds, maybe thousands of opportunities have you had to improve an existing relationship? You have no idea of the number because you've probably never given much thought before now and that's normal. Safe to say, it's probably a big number. This is not a cost in dollars. It's worse. It's a human cost for not being present.

Howa about at work? Haven't we all heard (and probably been first hand eye witness to) work stories of colleagues not *being present*?

Ask any four-fingered guy in the construction trades. He will tell you. There are thousands of examples of work-related injuries and deaths because people did not pay attention. They were distracted and therefore not being present.

Have you been in the meeting when the one Not Present gets called upon for a response or feedback? Wasn't their response painful to listen to and to watch them when they couldn't answer because they weren't paying full attention? You know there WAS a cost to them and their career and professional credibility. They weren't paying attention. They weren't present.

I don't wanna be "that guy" but trust me – I've BEEN "that guy".

You've probably seen the same things happen. I've seen people get reprimanded and even fired on the spot. Can you imagine having to go home and tell your spouse you lost your job for the same reason they get ticked off at you? You weren't paying attention. You weren't *being present,* and it cost you and MORE than just you.

What has it cost you and you didn't even know it?

What has not *being present* cost you and you didn't even know it? For me, I wonder if I might have a better relationship with my kids if *being present* had been more important to me earlier in my life. I wonder what not being present cost me in my relationship with them. Would they look up to me more? Would they trust me more? Would we have different conversations? Would we have a stronger bond? Could I help them more? Would they love me more?

I wonder what it cost THEM in terms of not getting feedback that may have been of great value to them (ouchies). Assuming I had parental feedback of value (most of us parents do) then when I am not present and don't engage, they won't get the benefit of what I have in my big old brain. Whose fault is that? Mine because I am the adult and I should know better. How many mistakes could I have possibly helped prevent?

Not connecting has a relationship cost and it is NOT only to us. That's the saddest part of realizing this reality. We're all familiar with the term "opportunity cost" when applied in a business environment. It's the cost of a missed opportunity whatever that opportunity is. It can most times be quantified and attached to a revenue number.

But HOW do you do calculate the opportunity cost of **not being present** in relationships? Much – Much – Much tougher and actually painful to consider.

Most of us have been emotionally touched by a loved one passing away. What would you give today to have been able to connect better with them when they were still here? Probably anything.

We all feel regret for the unspoken emotions – that's normal. But what about knowing you had a deeper more meaningful relationship when they were here because you engaged with them differently? Differently because you were present. (yeah – I'm tearing up at the thought also)

Now what about for all the others who are STILL HERE?

What have we ALL lost in relationship opportunity costs with our kids, our siblings, our parents and other family, our friends and our colleagues?

The truth is standing here today we don't know what NOT being present has cost us with these groups of people we care about. What I DO know and want you to believe is that going forward, it can be remarkably better!

You CAN make a difference very quickly and as your belief level and skills improve you will see a difference in those relationships. Some of those relationship include people who have less time than others in this world. That's a good enough reason to read a few more pages, right?

Takeaways:

- Understand that NOT being present has already cost you personally and professionally no matter who you are.
- Understand that you have an obligation to the people you care about to be present. They deserve it.
- You need to make an attempt to understand the cost of not being present in each of the relationships you value. Literally go down a list of those people. Some have less time on this

earth than others. Some may have a more urgent need than others.

- You need to decide to recognize and acknowledge the past behavior and then dismiss it and focus on what you can do today to improve these relationships. Don't beat yourself up – just be better.

Quote:

"Do not dwell in the past, do not dream of the future, concentrate the mind on the present moment."

-- Buddha

14 - NO MORE ABSENT EXPERIENCES

Another advantage of **Being Present** is that you don't have absent experiences. You don't have those experiences where you should be in the moment and you've mentally drifted somewhere else and therefore miss out!

Food Tastes Better – because you actually taste it. When was the last time you ate and ONLY ate? You didn't have two or three other things going on at the same time. You weren't listening to Pandora, Netflix chilling, watching reality TV, Instagram surfing or picking up email. You actually tasted and appreciated what you were eating and drinking. Maybe awhile?

When you are *being present* Music Sounds Better - because you're only listening. If there was an appreciation scale you can bet your sweet bippy that music listened to with no distractions would appear higher on it. You hear, appreciate, perceive and catch more of the detail. They say that behind every favorite song is a story. You just need to stop peddling your mental bike long enough to remember it.

When you are *being present* Nature Exists Again – and you can actually appreciate what you see, hear and smell when you are not distracted with those ear buds! You can look around and rediscover our big, beautiful world. Whether you are with someone else at the time or just alone, it's a great way to enjoy the beauty of the third rock from the sun.

When you are *being present* You Can See What You See – when you actually pause and look. When you visually absorb. When you aren't looking FOR something else, you can actually notice the details that you weren't tuned into before. Things about people like their moods, their facial expressions, their stress or their smiles. Details in clothes, cars, natural patterns, indoor and outdoor spaces, the weather and a thousand other things. I'll bet that you will almost always see something that has always been there a little differently.

When you are *being present* You Smell More - of your one trillion Olfactory Stimuli opportunities. Science Magazine report 343 reports that the human nose can detect one trillion distinct smells. Which ones might you be missing out on when you're mentally absent? *Smell ya later homie.*

When you are *being present* You Consume - with your senses- when you are quiet. When you are there just to experience instead of participating. What do you pick up on that you didn't have a chance to understand before because you were wrapped up in being busy and a participant?

When you are *being present* at nighty-night time, you sleep better. You can look up the science behind it but distractions like music and TV's prevent you from getting into the deep sleep zone we all need.

In short, God gave you senses to utilize – use them, don't be absent – be present.

Takeaways:

- Absent experiences suck. Since you control it - try not to have them. With a little focus you can change how often you are absent and enjoy life again.

- Stay in the moment and treat the thing you are doing or experiencing with the importance it deserves. Even if you are just taking a walk – JUST take a walk.
- Try being present with an individual sense and see what you notice.

Quote:

"Yesterday is history, tomorrow is a mystery, today is God's gift, that's why we call it the present." – Joan Rivers

15 - INCREASED ENGAGEMENT

Being Present means a higher level of engagement in all situations than was previously there. Make no mistake – engagement is a choice. There is a lot of information out there regarding engagement and what it means, how it applied, how and why you want to increase it. As it relates to the subject of ***being present***, I want to share engagement in the context of two focus areas, which are emotional and physical.

But first – I shall babble...
At its core, engagement is one of the easiest skills to improve. You will see results faster here than in many of the other focus areas of this book. If you want to increase the level of your personal engagement all you have to do is pay attention. Not to me or anything in this book, just pay attention. Just **be present**. That's it! Sure, there's a little more in the details but at the core, it's just that simple. You could not read another word in this book and just commit to paying attention better than you ever have and you will have nailed it!

A Couple of Benefits

Comprehension and retention of information goes up with higher level of engagement. It's true whether that is in a personal or work environment. There is a tremendous amount of supporting research on this subject and has had impact in many areas like how people are trained.

Satisfaction level goes up with whatever it is you are doing. When you've removed the distractions and are "in it" for whatever that "it" is your satisfaction increases.

Emotional Engagement

First, in my approach in these examples, I will assume that this is a valuable relationship and my role is to honor that. Whether it is an old friendship or maybe a new one, it has value to me. That said, there is no reason my approach would be different with anyone else who wasn't an old or new friend. Create the habit that honors the relationship.

I have to make a conscious effort to ask myself:

What is this person trying to communicate to me?
Why is it important to them?
Know my role at this moment is to be a "learner" and pick up on what IS said and also what is NOT said.
What clarifying questions should I ask?

If they are sharing a problem with me...

Are they looking for advice?
Are they specifically NOT looking for advice? Are they just looking for a nonjudgmental ear?

Physical Engagement

When I use the phrase physical engagement, I mean it to include the energy associated with how I physically listen and engage. Everything from the words I use to the voice inflection, eye contact, posture, leaning in, etc.

My Springer Parting Thought (yeah that dates me) is that engagement is the END result of an intentional effort to **be present**. Sneaky way to work that in there huh?

Takeaways:

- Engagement is a choice. Choose wisely!
- Comprehension and retention of information increases when you are being present.
- Figure out what this person really wants from this interaction and deliver it.
- Use a list if you have to initially until it is a habit.
- Learn and use the right physical cues to signal someone you are engaged.

Quote:

The other day a man asked me what I thought was the best time of life. "Why," I answered without a thought, "now." -- David Grayson

16 - WHO IS MOST IMPORTANT?

Who is MOST Important to **Be Present** With?
I know it's important with family, extended family, my friends, my
co-workers, my _____.

My bias is to say everyone equally. The reality is that none of us can
actually do that. If everyone is "most important" then no one really
is. The good news is that this is a journey and the goal should be to
simply do a little better each day with as many people as we can.
That's important to understand. This is the marathon not the sprint
in behavior changes. "A little better each day" is the call of EVERY
day. Nothing more is required.

You MAY already be cooking up a list of folks you know you've been
guilty of not being present with. That's good. Write those names
down. You will want them later!

Opinion Time: (but really, isn't all of this basically my opinion?)
Sure we may improve our abilities for all interactions and have more
productive relationships but if I (me personally) had to choose one
group, it would be with our children.

It is probably where we drop the ball MOST because we can without
catching too much flack. They aren't calling us out on our negligent
behavior because they don't know any better. We can get away with it
and we do. Let's face it they're shorter than we are and have
bedtimes!

Our kids are probably the single audience who NEED it most. One of our biggest jobs as parents is to build self-esteem in our kids and not ***being present*** does the opposite of that.

They are definitely the audience who DESERVES it most. Our kids warrant that devoted attention. They are worthy of it and we should honor that.

If I could do one thing in my life best, it would be to make a difference in the life of a child.

Take Aways:

- Your/Our kids are the most deserving of our efforts to be present.
- If you aren't blessed with kids then still figure out a way to engage with other family kids, neighbors or some that are in need. You don't a pass here!
- Get just the smallest bit better each and every day at being present with everyone.

Quote:

"Normal day, let me be aware of the treasure you are. Let me learn from you, love you, bless you before you depart. Let me not pass you by in quest of some rare and perfect tomorrow. Let me hold you while I may, for it may not always be so. One day I shall dig my nails into the earth, or bury my face in the pillow, or stretch myself taut, or raise my hands to the sky and want, more than all the world, your return."

-- Mary Jean Iron

17 - BEING PRESENT WITH KIDS

My Failure

I would tell what life-failure number this next subject matter is for me, but I stopped counting when my number of failures hit four digits (no decimal).

A bad story: I am sure I'm not the only Dad on the planet who has a son who likes video games. He likes football ones, fighting ones and even one where he can shoot a thousand other bad guys with about twelve different guns. I know what you're thinking, he sounds like one of a kind. He is. Well imagine me as the Dad who is always asked by his kid to play the games with him. I dutifully sit and kind of play but it's clear early on in each and every game that I don't have a chance. I'd like to blame it on my newfound discovery that I have opposable thumbs – but alas. I just suck at these games!

Meanwhile I'm drawing some gratification from being able to tell myself we spent quality time together playing games when in reality I was only ever **partially** there. I was kind of playing but with the list of things I didn't get done that day bouncing around my cerebellum and an ear tuned to the sound my phone makes on vibrate on a hardwood floor, I wasn't really *Being Present*. Well, at least he didn't pick up on it. Or did he?

So his Mom comes in and says "Hey that's great – you guys are playing a game together". (I'm thinking – oooh I get extra credit!)

To which my son innocently says, "Yeah he plays between calls." He wasn't mad, he was just stating the facts as he experienced them. BAMMMM! Gut punch in the Dad- plexis.

So he DID notice,... and for once – so did I.

How hard would it really have been for me to leave the phone in the other room? Why couldn't I just stop for 30 minutes and focus on him and our time together? Why couldn't I turn off the distractions in my head / give myself permission to "come back to those things later" and just be present?

Worse yet – what am I teaching him?

I hope this doesn't sound familiar, but I'll bet it does.

Kids Are Always Present

Kids are ALWAYS Present. It's their only option and the only way they can be. They can't multi-task and they don't want to. It's the furthest thing from their excited little minds! They get incredible enjoyment from what they are doing at that moment and even more if it somehow includes sugar!

They ARE present and focused on their friend, that puppy, that ball or that game or whatever that ONE thing is. They aren't thinking about what happened yesterday or might happen tomorrow or even dinner tonight. They are ALL IN right now! COWABUNGA Dudes!!!!

And that feeling lasts until we, and life drive it out of them. Till we make them grow up and pay attention to their surroundings because we want them to be safe (stranger danger) or whatever that other thing is.

If you want to see **Being Present** in its purest form as natural behavior – watch kids play. Just watch and listen and enjoy.

If you're lucky enough to get invited to engage then DO IT! Get on the ground and see what they see. Step back a few years and actually play. I'd bet you would find that you get more than they do from **being present** in that situation.

Another observation for me now that I've been more aware is that you can't really fool kids. They learn and mirror to such an incredible degree before age three it's mind-boggling. Their skills and knowledge grow exponentially from there. They KNOW when adults fake it. Fake interest, fake participation, and fake whether they are actually enjoying the time. Here I say "be careful" because you don't want to miss out. Kids of all ages gravitate to real attention and engagement. Hey, guess what they're just really just like us aren't they?

Take Aways:

• Kids are the most important people to be present with. • You can't really fool kids.
• Kids don't behave any other way than **being present**.

Quote:

"Children have neither a past nor a future. Thus, they enjoy the present – which seldom happens to us."
-- Jean de la Bruyère

18 - BEING PRESENT AT HOME

What is the family culture you have created or allowed to happen inside your home? Is it a representation that you are proud of?

Maybe it's great already or maybe it's worth looking at a little deeper. Whatever it looks like – it's a reflection of you and what you have made most important in your home. Sometimes it's what you have ALLOWED to be represented as most important in your home by default. Sometimes your family culture represents the default position of "what's left". What's left after everything else is "handled". Are you uncomfortable yet? You probably should be and that's normal too.

Would you guess that a faith-based culture in your home is the solution? It helps in many other areas but not in this one. No type of home is immune.

We all have created intentionally or by default the culture in our homes.

Are you the one who handles the household? Are you the Head of the Household? I've always thought the phrase "Head of Household" was interesting. The assumption is that it is the tall, breadwinning King of the Castle. In reality, who would you guess actually runs the household most of the time? OK – so now I have the ladies on my side! My actual point is gender neutral.

It doesn't matter what your role is in the home, it only matters that when you're there – you're there. And you also have the responsibility to **define and uphold** the culture of your home. After all – if you don't who will - your partner? Well if you both believed you "owned" the responsibility the likelihood of it actually executing it goes up dramatically.

What do you think each person who lives with you REALLY wants from you? How do you feel you do at fulfilling those wants? Are you proud? I haven't been. I know I've failed. I'd give myself a "C" at best. I've failed at the hello's, goodbyes, good mornings, good nights, and the thousand things in between. Maybe you have also.

Do you want to change your family culture to something stronger and more meaningful? Something you can really hand down from generation to generation? Hand down because it will be part of the DNA and fabric of your family structure.

Being Present at home will help you connect in those most important of relationships and in a more meaningful way.

Wanna start? Ask yourself and your spouse these questions:
What do I really want those family and individual experiences in my home to be like?
How do I want the people I have the largest moral obligation to affect positively, to feel?
What would I want a home where I AM present, to look and feel like?

Part of changing the culture in your own home is the effort to "begin with the end in mind". Your intent should be to make an effort to honor the values you hold high and see them manifested in your home and in those relationships you value. Hopefully you have already defined those values.

It's Us Against Them!

It's the parents against the hungry, smelly, unappreciative tax deductions dressed up like our kids!

If you're fortunate to be one half of a two-parent household smile now and you're your spousal unit a big kiss. This concept is easier to execute when both of "the rents" are onboard. There is the obvious relationship value to each other but true gold in the mutual accountability of creating a "***being present*** at home" environment.

In many home situations, we really don't have the chance to spend a lot time with our families. The time windows are small and as you already know, full of other activities and distractions.

If you have children and depending on their age, there are pick-ups and drop-offs, transit time, meals, health stuff, etc. It's a crazy long list of things to get done every day. You're probably just happy to be able to get all the to-do boxes checked! Their lives end up being just as busy as ours. On a different subject – sometimes fewer more meaningful activities in our children's lives is better (just say'in).

"If it is to be, it is up to me." Has never been more true, than here. Assuming you have a two-parent home, your best shot is getting your spousal unit on board. *"it takes two to make a thing go riiiigghhttt"* – thank you Rob Base and DJ EZ Rock.

There are four basic steps.

Step 1 is to get alignment on the resources – you and your spousal unit!

If there are two parents, it will take both and more importantly won't work when you have only one of two engaged. This is critical.

Step 2 is Clarity of the Objective.

What are you trying to accomplish in your home? You gotta put this on paper and make it visible. Everything else will be a Strategy or Tactic of that Objective. If it doesn't support the Objective, it doesn't make the list. This is where people make the mistake of falling in love with a Strategy or a Tactic and end up with very unproductive activities. It's bad enough that it is done poorly in business every day, but you can't allow it to happen in your home where it is even more important! Take a look at a good example below which is targeted at a family that includes kids that can talk – ha ha!

Objective
"We want to create an environment where time spent with parts or all of the family are times of engagement. Times where we are all *being present*."

Strategy - 1
Find ways around meal times to reduce distractions.

Tactic – 1
No cell phone rule

Tactic – 2
Everyone eats together

Tactic – 3
No TV's or distracting sounds

Strategy - 2
Discuss things you think are important AND silly stuff.

Tactic – 1

How was your day / test / event / etc.

Tactic – 2
Instead of telling kids how they should feel ask them how that thing did make them feel. Dig deeper and understand before you impart your all-knowing wisdom.

Tactic – 3
Anything funny happen today? Here's my story. Who can beat it that story?

The strategies and all of the tactics support the overall objective of "We want to create an environment where time spent with parts or all of the family are times of engagement. Times where we are all **being present.**"

If the strategy or tactic don't support the objective... DO NOT let it make your list!

Step 3 – Plan for the Pain.

This kind of effort will probably not be received well initially no matter what you say, but there is one thing you can do to make it easier. Communicate the "why" to everyone who is affected.

- Why do we want to do this?
- Why we think it is important?
- What is the value in it?
- What is the benefit to the family as a whole?
- Why should you participate?
- What is the benefit to you?

This the best way to explain the value in this "Begin with the end in mind" approach.

Step 4 – Review, Revise and Repeat

Review - Mom and Dad should review the interactions and make sure you have alignment on what you perceived. The train can get off the tracks right here if your takeaways are opposite of each other. Make the time to review as quickly after the interaction as possible. I know a couple who kept index cards handy to make notes in case it was going to a few hours before they could chat privately.

Revise – Determine of your approach, questions, etc. should be changed. You can change a Strategy or a Tactic but NOT the Objective. Based on what went or felt right what should you continue to do? Based on what felt like it went wrong what should you modify? Notice I didn't say get rid of, I said modify. Maybe the subject matter is very important to the effort, but you flubbed up the way you handled it. No biggie – just find a better way to say or do it.

Repeat – Keep the rhythm. Be consistent and don't miss doing it this way. Not even once! There is tremendous value in the trust placed in Mom's and Dad's for doing things the same way for their kids. This is a new habit that has layers of emotional security that your kids deserve. Don't let them down!

How do you know if it is working?
If you are like most families, your will know VERY quickly. In fact, during the first week! The value increases over time though. With the rhythm consistency and as conversation content moves from surface to deeper, you will see, hear and feel it. You will end up with the family culture you are proud of. The one you created versus just let happen. (dem dere are powerful words)

Last but not least – this concept extends to ***being present*** with family in other people's homes. You may be interacting with them in a home other than your own. Maybe it's another family members home or another gathering place. No matter where it is, the value is still the same.

Takeaways:

- Your family culture is what you've allowed to happen whether you planned for it to happen that way or not.
- These are the most important people in your world.
- *"it takes two to make a thing go riiiigghhttt"*
- Follow the Objective, Strategies and Tactics structure.
- Plan for the pain and explain the WHY.
- Keep the rhythm of Review, Revise, Repeat.

Quote:

"Love the moment, and the energy of the moment will spread beyond all boundaries."

- Corita Kent

19 - BEING PRESENT AT WORK (YOU ARE THE EMPLOYEE)

Q: Is it important to Be Present at work?
A: Only if you like receiving a paycheck so you can live indoors.

Do you recognize this guy?

Mr. (or Mrs.) Multi-tasker – super busy, very important, juggles a lot of balls and doesn't mind you knowing it. It's obvious as you can see his iPhone or Droid never leaves his person. He would Velcro it to his hand if he could. He gets a lot done – he thrives on the constant stream of information coming in and going out from himself. He's an activity-junkie and doesn't even know it. With him, it's not about being effective; it's about being busy. Never bored, always in demand. Uses his laptop in meetings to take notes (yeah – rriiiggghhhtttt), has his face in his phone instead of the person speaking. Badda-boom, badda-bing, ker-ching!

Part of his problem is that he's made himself "within reach" in many mediums and on many devices including office e-mail, personal e-mail(s), Face Book, Linked-In, and a couple dozen opt-in retail or social notifiers.

He has said "I'm ALWAYS available" and has set that expectation for contact and responses. AND unless addressed, he has also set expectations for those around them to ACCEPT the interrupted behavior. You might ask "How is that bad?" It doesn't have to be as long as you aren't perusing e-mail in the middle of a meeting or a conversation whether it's voice-to-voice or face-to-face or even worse – while driving.

How many times have YOU been talking to someone else on the phone about something important to you and when it is their time to respond you hear that pause and a get a feeble reply and you know they are doing something else in addition to conversing with you?

How about when you are talking, and you can actually hear them typing out something on their computer. You KNOW you don't have their full attention. They are NOT Present. You are getting something less (who knows how much less) than was your intent when you entered the conversation.

It is that old "hearing" versus "listening" paradox.
How many times has it come back to bite someone in the details or follow up? I'll bet you have a dozen stories (I have a few hundred) that come to mind immediately. Have you ever said, "Yes we did talk about that yesterday on the phone and I told you
_____"?

Doesn't it feel like they are brushing you off like emotional dandruff? Ouch – that kinda hurts right?

If you are looking for a way to set yourself apart from your colleagues... THIS IS IT.

You have probably heard the phrase "Good is the enemy of Great". What is also true is that multi-tasking is the enemy of *Being Present*. The truth is that as humans, you cannot EFFECTIVELY do multiple things at once. You cannot even do TWO of those things at once. The difference will ultimately be "a dilution of your effectiveness". Less truly is, more.

The Myth of Multitasking

The myth of multi-tasking is that you are MORE productive. There is a great book by Dave Crenshaw called *The Myth of Multitasking* I'd suggest you read if you intend to change the culture of your work teams.

Being Present is what happens when you are NOT trying to multi-task.

The practical business execution of ***Being Present*** happens when you are being intentional, being focused.

There is a lot of information out there that suggests that people who multi-task aren't more productive. They just feel better about what they are doing. There is a huge difference. Media multi-tasking is even worse. Media multi-tasking is the layering on of different forms of media. An example would be that I am sending emails while I am watching something on my iPad and getting phone notifications that I check.

Setting Yourself Apart

It's been said that companies all over the world are suffering from a lack of valuing their human capital. That there's no job security and that companies just don't care. That people are just human commodities. In many cases that may be true but certainly not in all. The business landscape has changed, and smart companies now know they have to appeal to the individual and what that individual takes gratification from. But how do YOU set yourself apart from the crowd and become noticed and appreciated at a higher level? Is what you are currently doing achieving what you want it to? Are you setting yourself apart?

How many of your co-workers are looking for ways to maintain their own marketability within the four walls of your company? (probably not enough of them) They don't even think about it, so YOU are already ahead!

How many of your co-workers fill the gaps of their needed fulfillment with Social Media rather than *being present* and asking, "how else can I add value?" The answer is probably not a small number and that's a shame.

So how do you set yourself apart? Being Present is one way. The best of the best interpersonal skills is ***Being Present***. If could go back to the beginning of my career and hone one skill, improve one personality trait, it would be this one.

It's simple. Do you want to be better at what you do? Do you want to add more NOTICEABLE value? **Be Present**!

Wouldn't you want the reputation of "that person who listens"? Do you think that people at ALL levels inside your company or outside in the business community would appreciate and notice your level of engagement? Of course they would.

Do you think that creates a favorable impression of you? Of course it does! If you are the same (***being present***) with all internal company audiences, then do you think everyone at ALL levels would think highly of you? I think you know the answer to this one.

Do you think the positive attributes and impressions created from ***Being Present*** would be especially helpful if your role were in Sales? Yeppers, pretty sure it does!

Do you think that as an employee it matters what your actual role is with regard to **being present?** The answer is no. No matter what you do for the company that pays you, you will be a better YOU and employee for these efforts.

Your production whether in volume OR quality of work OR thinking will improve! I have never seen even ONE instance where it has not improved when the effort is there.

Q: So, what can you do?
A: Reduce your distractions and practice *being present*.

Look for ways to reduce distractions in your individual workspace. Now read on into the next chapter if you want some insight into what employers should be doing on the same subject. Who knows maybe you will even be able to have some influence there.

Takeaways:

• It's important to be present at work. People are counting on you.
• Manage your distractions. It helps.
• Don't even try to multi-task. It doesn't REALLY work.
• Set yourself apart. Earn a NEW reputation.

Quote:

"Living in the present moment creates the experience of eternity." – Deepak Chopra

20 - GROWING TOP PERFORMERS AT WORK (YOU ARE THE EMPLOYER)

Heads up Sparky! If you are in a leadership role – this one is for you. Read it twice!!

How do you use the concept of **Being Present** to improve performance in the work environment?
Think of it first like this. What is the opposite of Being Present? Being distracted right? Whether the distraction was created intentionally by the team member or post creation was never stopped, it's still a distraction. It still prevents the team member from **Being Present** and focusing the best of their talents and skills to the task at hand.

Guess who *"owns"* that problem and solution. That's right, YOU do!

The initial approach to growing top performers at work is through *"programming"*. You are programming environments to get the end result you want. You *"Begin With the End in Mind"* and direct your efforts to create the steps in the environment to get the result you want. The result becomes more predictable. Everybody wins.

Small Left Turn: *"Begin With the End in Mind"* is a phrase I use often, and it really means stop now and make sure that the actions you are about to take are going to lead you to your desired END result. So many times in my life my actions would have been different if only I had hit "pause" and thought though where my next steps would lead. That's true in my personal relationships and in my business life. It's become such an important part of how I think now that I keep the first letter of each of those words (BWTEIM) written at the top of paper I write on or white boards or notecards or anyplace I can see it. The concept anchors me in good behavior.

The Leaders Focus

The two areas of focus should be Environmental Programming and Cultural Programming. You will likely get 20% of your results through the Environmental portion and 80% from the Cultural portion.

Environmental Programming

This refers to the physical environment where the body of work is to be done.

Your role is to remove the distraction obstacles and make it easier for the team member to *be present* and accomplish their contributing body of work. There are thousands of examples of what this may look like depending on the industry and application. Once that is done the environment is naturally going to be an easier please to remain focused in.

This exercise is basically the same as what big box retailers spend millions of dollars in research to figure out. They want to program the environment to get the most favorable result from a potential customer. They consider lighting, music, odors, temperature, space set-up, travel paths, merchandising and a ton of other data points. We won't have to go nearly as in depth for what we will do. We are just trying to remove obstacles for our team members!

Here are a few considerations to help your team members to be present. These can apply no matter what your SIC (Standard Industry Classification) code or work environment is.

Start by thinking of a few of your senses.

Do, Re, Mi, Fa, So, La, Ti, NO

Sound – What do your team members hear? What is the ambient noise? Do team members hear each other's conversations? Do they hear customers' conversations that are not their customers? This can be all over the board depending on your industry and individual team member roles. Even in some sales and customer service environments where it is thought to be an advantage to be able to hear and learn from others you lose more benefit than you gain.

I hate even saying this because I love music so much but there is a lot of cognitive research that makes it clear that music hampers memory tasks, calculations and attention to detail. So NO to the background music and even the white noise machines. NO also to team members being allowed to wear earbuds. Well that's not going to make me popular!

The research does vary depending on the desired output of your role. If your role is specifically to be creative, then music is thought to be a plus.

Sight – What do they see? Is there visual noise or distractions? Sit where they sit or stand where they stand and travel their path to the normal destinations in a day. If in an office environment walk to the kitchen/break room, to the restroom, to the other offices they have to travel. Are they visually bombarded? What could be removed OR replaced to make it easier to not be distracted.

Smell – This may seem unimportant, but I've heard of people who are not only less productive because of the smells they are exposed to but who actually change jobs as a result. That's extreme but you probably wouldn't want the cubicle just outside the Men's restroom either.

I'm not recommending a fragrance-free workplace policy, which seems to be on the rise but are there odors that need to be neutralized because they are distracting!

Smell is actually the strongest of all of the senses and able to influence brain activity. If you decide to not to have a fragrance-free work environment, then jump on the growing business bandwagon considering aromatherapy. Advertising agency creatives are enjoying the smell of peppermint in their shnoz to help them be better at being creative! Same is true for many companies who have brainstorming sessions.

Other specific fragrances known to help fight mental fatigue, improve focus, memory and concentration are Cinnamon, Jasmine, Rosemary, Lavender and Lemon. If you decide to go down this path, do your own research and find one or two options to try.

Absenteeism

A few years ago, there was a Harvard Business Review article that summarized benefits of organizations with a focused effort on employee engagement. I draw the correlation between a team member who is **being present** to one who is engaged to say that you reap very similar rewards.

The article referenced a Gallop Survey that included 1.4 million employees. Some relevant takeaways were:

- Lower absenteeism
- 22% higher productivity
- 48% fewer safety incidents
- 41% fewer defect or quality incidents

- In high turnover organizations a 25% reduction in turnover
- In low turnover organizations a 65% reduction in turnover

Pretty impressive right? Most employers would say they would whatever it takes to have some of those results. Here are some additional considerations.

Safety

Research shows that engaged employees have a substantially decreased chance of experiencing an accident. Engaged employees (those that are *being present*) are as much as four times less likely than their counterparts to have a safety incident and seven times less likely to have a lost-time incident. There are studies that found disengaged employees are nearly twice as likely to be injured on the job as their engaged counterparts. If you work in a manufacturing or heavy equipment environment, this is especially important. Soooooooo....... When we are engaged in what we do we tend to follow safety procedures more diligently and don't lose focus as often, thus leading to fewer safety incidents. Simply put – **being present** is being safer.

Health

Want to improve your team members overall health? One study monitored a group of 168 engaged and disengaged workers multiple times during a day to measure stress, as well as other health indicators. Those that were *being present* reported lower stress and higher interest levels throughout the day. They also showed improvements in cholesterol and blood pressure.

Happiness

Employees who are *being present* and happiness may be closely related but are not the same. Employees can be happy but not being present in their work. But those who are *being present* in what they do are much more likely to also be happy. So, don't worry, be happy AND be present!

Productivity

Your employees actually have a desire to be measured. Why would you guess that is? Because they want what we all want which is to be recognized!

Much of the research on employee engagement shows that engaged employees perform better than their peers. Engaged employees not only work harder, but also work smarter and are able to produce better results. Isn't that what you want as an employer?
This also helps them to earn higher wages, receive faster promotions, and market themselves for better career opportunities. Many people describe being engaged as "having an awesome day at work," or "being in the zone." Being fully engaged allows them to get more out of their workday while feeling positive and energized.

Cultural Programming (the other 80%)

Same as with environmental programming your role is to remove the distraction obstacles and make it easier for the team member to *be present*.

Question: How would you guess employees who are *being present* at work might be described or perceived?
Answer: Intentional, focused, driven, high performers, happy, positive, confident and organized?

Isn't that what you want your team to look like? Are you programming the team to look like that?

This is EXACTLY the same concept as when I asked earlier in this book if your family culture represented something you were proud of. If it doesn't – you own it. If it kinda does but still misses many marks, then you own the result of the gaps because YOU haven't done your part. Those unattended gaps by the way naturally become bigger over time and that's NOT a good thing.

So how do you do that as a leader in your organization? Do two things exceptionally well. Create Clarity and Remove Obstacles. Whether you are a senior team member, a manager or executive this should be something you make important in your company. Doing it right will allow your team members to do fewer things better (critical) and measure them. When you are able to draw the favorable picture of what *being present* looks like at work, they will WANT to be that thing! When you are able to describe what it feels like – they will be onboard! They want to be in that club or group of people who are winning and feeling good about it.

So, no matter your individual role, mentally put on that leader jacket and be prepared to do what leaders do. Let's look at these two initiatives and how integrating them into your culture helps your team members **be present** and benefit.

3. Create Clarity
   When I say create clarity, I specifically mean that there are no unanswered questions regarding expectations. This should quickly become the foundation of your culture. These would include who we are as a company, the direction we are headed and why, how we agree to operate internally in terms of execution and individual interactions (behaviors) and what the performance expectations are to name a few.

VERY important is how we are expected to react to positive (always overlooked) and negative performance variances.

Benefit to the Team Member – My distractions are fewer because I have the peace of mind that comes from this clarity. I don't wonder what the REAL intent is or scenario play because I am clear. It saves me a lot of productive time and frees up a lot of mental space. I don't have to guess what the targets are, or which thing is more important than which other thing. I am clear and therefore it is easier for me to *be present*.

Benefit to the Organization – Your team members are focused on fewer more impactful things that reinforce your culture. A culture of clarity gives YOU the best chance of achieving your objectives. If you think you already have clarity in your culture, I'd ask you to validate that with some challenge questions of your team.

Start at the bottom position of the organization and ask team members at each level going up specific questions that would validate that they are clear. My guess is that you will have some (who knows how many) team members that aren't clear.
The good news is that you can now turn this into a culture opportunity and your entire organization will benefit. Why? When Team Members are clear it is easier for them to *be present*.

4. Remove Obstacles
   When I say Remove Obstacles, I specifically mean removing anything and everything that is between your Team Member and them being able to achieve the desired result. This is another foundational pillar of your culture that helps Team Members *be present*.

This can include real operating system sticking points where problems continue, needed tools or training, removing organizational terrorists (bad people) or poor performers, dysfunctional communication and fifty others. You have to be open and ask your team to get the list started once they understand the objective.

Benefit to the Team Member – "I recognize an issue and instead of living with it and complaining about it I always know I can bring it up. It will get attention because leadership wants to make it easier for me to do my job. They know I am more productive when I have fewer internal issues to deal with so I can *be present*."

I'm comfortable bringing up opportunities to improve.

Benefit to the Organization – When leadership removes obstacles, they enjoy a higher sense of confidence and trust from team members. That increases with each triumph. When team members have a forum to ask for and receive help the organization wins whether the ultimate solution is what the team member thought it should be or not. In the end, the team member is no longer focused on (or distracted by) the obstacle. They can **be present**.

Takeaways:

You CAN use Being Present to improve results in your business. Focus on Environmental Programming (20%) and Cultural Programming (80%) Commit to Creating Clarity and Removing Obstacles

Quote:

"Do not dwell in the past, do not dream of the future, concentrate the mind on the present moment." – Buddha

21 - BEING PRESENT AND GOD... OR WHOEVER

(Yeah – bout to go a little religio on ya!)

I'm a Christian but it doesn't really matter who I or you pray to. You probably also believe in a higher power. Feel free to insert any other name of religion where I use Christian or God below.

Question: What would you guess is the life experience a caring and loving God wants for you?

Answer: I believe it is for you to "be good" and "of good to others". I believe the simplicity of that is a life truism. I also believe that you can be neither without **Being Present**. (that's BIG)

So because I believe that answer, I believe I am closer to God when I am present. I am better prepared to be open, to receive the messages, to be guided, to be shown, to "feel the reveal". Being present in this way means allocating time with the RIGHT intent. The first part of that is to be intentional about allocating time to spend with God. I love my church (North Point Community Church locations– shout out to Andy and teams!) but I enjoy my time there because of the music, the fellowship and the things I learn. I devote other time to **being present** with God. I look for other ways to put his word in front of me so that I can be present in it and closer to him.

Can I call myself a Christian or Jesus follower and not Be Present? Certainly, I can but I may not be able to be the BEST that I could be OR gain the most from my personal relationship with God.

If I am not present, then I may NOT able to be "as good" as I can be

for me. I'm probably not as open or spiritually available. I've recently described myself in that scenario when I was younger and said, "If God called, he'd would have gotten a busy signal." It's truly a "must be present to win" experience.

Example:
Have you heard the message from airline attendants when explaining what to do in the event of having to use an oxygen mask? They say to place the mask over your own face first and then over the face of your child or traveling companion.

The reason for placing it over your face first is simple. If you can't breathe your opportunity to help those you care about is limited. If you can't "be good" then your opportunity to be "of good to others" is limited.

To be clear, NOT being able to maximize my opportunity to "be good" also by extension means I cannot be AS "of good to others" as I have the capacity to be. These are inherently linked.

I believe that my God wants me to be less Mind Full of noise and more Mindful of the opportunity to be closer to his true intent. Basically, **_Being Present_** to "be good" and "of good to others".

I truly want to be... "Gooder"!

I want to Be Present in those times, those spaces and places to receive that spiritual nutrition from my God that helps me be a better me for myself and others.

I would ask you to consider what this concept could mean to you in your spiritual journey. Is there something here in this message that resonates with you and that you could use? Maybe something you need? Maybe something that you would consider trying? You have nothing to lose and I believe, a tremendous amount to gain. Pray about it!

Quote:

"Therefore do not worry about tomorrow, for tomorrow will worry about itself. Each day has enough troubles of its own." Matthew 6:24, Jesus Christ

22 - WHEN IS IT OK TO NOT BE PRESENT?

LOT'S of times. As a general rule anytime you are a casual observer versus needing to be an engaged participant. Hey when I'm at the breakfast table watching TV, surfing on my iPad, answering texts on my phone and buttering my mail, I know I'm gonna miss something or make a mistake and that's OK. I have grown fond of the taste of butter (not margarine) on my mail.

I'm not completely present when I'm watching reruns of *The Daily Show* or *In the Kitchen with David* or at a cookout, or some sporting events (except Braves games of course) or grocery shopping. It's OK because it's not as critical to have the same level of engagement.

You can't be singularly focused every minute of every day. That's not what this concept is about. It's about **being present** when you NEED to be, not all the time.

When you're in those relaxing or escapism times just enjoy them. Hey when I'm watching a movie, I'm just watching a movie. I may be present by default because I'm enjoying it but it's not because I'm making a conscious effort to be. Nobody is depending on me to engage.

Takeaways:

• You don't have to be present all the time. (you really don't want to be)

• Casual observers need to relax too!

Quote:

"Unease, anxiety, tension, stress, worry — all forms of fear — are caused by too much future, and not enough presence. Guilt, regret, resentment, grievances, sadness, bitterness, and all forms of nonforgiveness are caused by too much past, and not enough presence." – Eckhart Tolle

23 - MY "FRIEND" NEEDS HELP

In this case, maybe it really is a friend.

The question is, "How do I help someone who I know really needs this information and could benefit from it?"

Step 1 – yeah you knew it was coming, BUY THEM THIS BOOK. (I like living indoors and having money for Starbucks.)

You know this is always tricky territory. If someone came to me and said "Hey – you've kinda got a problem and you need help. Here – read this book." – They're not likely to get my best response. I kind of think I'd like to spew my mouthful of coffee on their shirt. You're probably not much different than me because being on the receiving end of a blame-thrower never feels good.

People are only willing to ACCEPT and VALUE criticism or feedback from someone whose motivations they trust. If they trust WHY you are telling them something, they are more likely to NOT be defensive and listen. Everyone I've ever met is the same in this regard. If you are in that truly trusted place with someone, you may have success with that approach.

But what about ALL the other people? What about your best friend, your co-worker, your boss, your neighbor, your Starbucks friends, church friends and YES, I'm saying it – your spousal unit (or wanna be spousal unit)?

Ahhhhh – so many questions, so few pages – I'll continue.

Here is an approach that a smarter person than me used ON ME and it worked. I was disarmed. They didn't make me feel defensive and sooooo I took the bait,... and I benefited. Here is how it went, and I'll bet YOU could make a difference in someone's life doing the same or something similar.

"Hey – don't know if you have any interest and you probably don't need it but I just finished this book and I want to pass it on to someone. They described me and my bad habits all through the book and it was kinda funny to see that. You wanna give it peek?"

Then let them know when they are through, they can *"Pass it back or pass it on"*.

Simple – Straightforward and Effective. It worked on me and the person who did it knew exactly what they were doing. It was an incredibly manipulative effort and also very kind that they CARED enough to figure out a way I would receive the message well. They knew I would be defensive, and they figured out a workaround. Well done friend – you know who you are!

If you want to make a difference in someone's life – try it. This Works!

Takeaways:

- Who do you know who needs to learn how to be present?
- What is the best way to get them to try it?
- Are you the best person to try to get them started or is there a better "messenger"?

Quote:

Life is a succession of moments. To live each one is to succeed. – Coreta Kent

24 - A SERVER STORY

I had a friend who was a stunningly attractive server with an incredible personality. She tried to convince me that her male customers wanted one thing even more than watching her bringing them their food. I was pretty sure I knew the answer to this one but as usual – I was wrong. She said it was her undivided attention. (I pretended to pay attention.) She said that when all of her other customers were taken care of, she enjoyed talking with folks because she just naturally enjoyed talking with people and learning more about them. She said she was frequently complimented about that trait. It was so appreciated by her customers that many said "It was great that you wanted to know more about me, my job, what I like to do, my family, my kids. You seemed focused on ONLY me. It was like no one else was around."

She told me that she had heard it many times. Then one day when the light bulb went off and she realized how appreciated that behavior really was, she poured even more effort into it. I guessed that it was easy because she was naturally wired that way (emotional DNA). She said that her tips became better and better.

She said that men truly appreciate a woman who is sincerely focused on them. Why? Because many times they don't get that intentional focus in other areas of their life. She suggests that is true. Not at work – not at home – not anywhere and she thinks that happens a lot. I asked her if she thought that might be true for women as well and said she was sure it was true for both genders.

Server wisdom – you can never underestimate it! The truth is that customer is no different than my Aunt Pat, your best friend or

anyone else on the planet. We ALL appreciate being around someone who is *being present*.

I understood that her enjoyment of interacting with people in general was just part of her natural personality. She had probably been that way all her life. The interesting thing was that when the light bulb went off and she realized the impact when she applied it to her work environment... it made a difference!

I wonder how most of us would react if we could double or triple our income by changing this one little thing. The jobs that have a more immediate Return On Being Present (ROBP?) see it faster I'm sure. What about all of the other types of jobs where the ROBP is slower? Is it still worth it? My answer of course would be YES. You don't have to be as smart as a server to understand that.

Takeaways:

• Some people naturally enjoy engaging with others.
• There is an emotional and sometimes a financial (ROBP) benefit to being present.
• Everyone has a history or herstory and they all want to tell it to you. How can you receive it better? Be Present and just listen and receive.
• Would there be a financial Return On Being Present (ROBP) in your job?

Quote:

"Life is a great and wondrous mystery, and the only thing we know that we have for sure is what is right here right now. Don't miss it."
-- Leo Buscaglia

25 - TRAINING YOURSELF TO BE PRESENT

You can train yourself to THINK differently about *Being Present*. As soon as you convince yourself that it's a good thing and that you want to do it because you see the value in it – your training has started!

It makes all the sense in the world to do it but how do you start?

A: You literally have to plan to be present until it is a fully formed habit. Then, NEVER stop practicing!

Here are some areas to include in your training:

Mentally

Be able to say, "You there – you have my attention. I've removed all the distractions I control. I am ready to engage."

Physically

Here are some things to try. It will take time but eventually they will become so natural you won't even know you are doing them.

Posture – Erect and forward (lean in) signals that you are interested. The challenge is that sitting erect for even 10 minutes can be a comfort challenge. The solution is a concept called "balanced seating" and you should look it up on that Google thingy for greater detail than I will give here. In short you are angling your posture as though your seat were tilted forward slightly. This will be more comfortable over time but will have you using new muscles initially, which will be sore. Take two ibuprofen and call me in the morning. Don't give up!

Body Direction – Face them. Don't movie theatre seat the interaction and sit beside them. They need to see you and you need to see them in order to get the best benefit from this. Ignore this if you are at a game. Be present THERE and just pray the Braves, Gators or Dolphins win! (go ahead – let the hating on me begin)

Distance – Close but not too close! If you are at a table, the distance is set. There are a lot of Social Distance studies out there, but the net is that the "Personal Zone" is 1.5 – 4 feet. I use that as my rule for when I'm talking with someone and our chairs are facing each other.

Facial Feedback – This should be a reflection of your emotional response to what you are hearing. Some people have to practice their *"are you pooping me face"* and others couldn't keep it off their face if they had to. You will find over time that you will *"give good face"* because you will see it in the other person. If you naturally have RBF you will have to make an extra effort, and this will be critically important for you.

Nod Ya Head – It's not always agreeing; it's sometimes just acknowledging that you heard what they said. Slow nodding shows you are engaged and also encourages them to continue. I over-nod and probably look like a human Pez dispenser. Don't be like me. Find your inner-nod rhythm and use it when you feel it.

Eye Contact – 50/70 Rule. Make eye contact 50% of the time when you are speaking and 70% of the time when you are listening. That may sound tough but it's not a blinking contest it's just eye contact. A big part of eye contact is maintaining the right amount of it. Too much gives the impression you're aggressive or even creepy, too little and you're not engaged. Have you ever been having coffee or lunch with the person who always has an eye on the restaurant door? Every time it opens, you lose them for two seconds while they check out whoever is coming in. They're not really engaged or *being present*. Don't be "that guy" unless you're Jason Bourne and you HAVE to constantly watch the door.

Touching? – Sure, just don't do anything that will get you arrested (insert LOL here). The hand on the arm or hand or shoulder is so incredibly impactful in terms of connecting. As humans, we connect so much by touch. Whenever you've gotten the literal pat on the back it felt really good didn't it? Same here. They will appreciate it and they will remember it.

Tilted Head – Yes Sparky, just like your dog does it! It can mean a lot of things but certainly shows you are giving what they said consideration. It may also prompt them to add detail when they see your reaction.

Be Still – When you're fidgety or moving frequently, it gives the other person the impression that you are not engaged (or have to pee really bad). The absence of movement makes them feel the opposite. You seem calm, cool and collected and you are not distracting.

Connection Words and Phrases

Much of this is not new at all. It may come off as salesy or manipulative, but it isn't. You committing to using it reflects your intent to engage in this effort for all the right reasons. Try these:

Reflecting or repeating part of what you think you've heard back to them as a confirmation. Don't overuse it or they will just think you're "slow".

Clarifying Questions – Should be used only when needed to confirm something so use them sparingly.

Train yourself to begin to work in some of these phrases and questions when appropriate. Remember the assumption is that they want to talk to you. You are just drawing out the content they want to tell you anyway.

I can tell... that bothers you or you like that or (fill in the blank)
That's interesting (if it is).
I never thought of that.
I didn't know that.

I like the way you said that. Tell me more about that. That's smart.

Open ended questions if they are not a follow up or clarification question. What would you do if _____?
Why do you think that?
Has that ever happened before?

What do you recommend?
How does that make you feel?
What makes you think that?
Tell me more about that.
Why did you pick _____?
What are you thinking best next steps are?

Do you have a Plan B?

Don't interrupt.
Anchor on "common ground" issues and comments.
Don't even THINK about complementing them unless it is sincere.

The Actual Training

How? – One way is to understand that you are just trying to affect a small change in many places in your life. That shouldn't feel like a daunting task. You are simply creating a new habit.

A good friend of mine has a saying that I like. He describes the secret to much of his personal and professional success as "small disciplines – repeated daily". This dude is successful, so I listen to what he says!

He says that "small disciplines – repeated daily" just means having the discipline to keep at it – whatever that IT is. He doesn't try to make or endorse making huge wholesale changes if you want to improve in a particular area. He says that there's more to be gained from consistently applying a small change than ANY one big change can give you. I believe him.

You have the "win" of seeing yourself consistently accomplish something and seeing it stick. That fuels a positive attitude about your ability to do it again. Your faith level in yourself is greater. Then you do just like the shampoo bottle says and "wash, rinse, repeat".

But what about that phrase? Small "disciplines". **Being Present** can become a discipline or habit but it will require practice. Fortunately, it's a pretty easy habit to create.

A very uninteresting factoid about me is that I loathe Acronyms. I mean the pompous way someone will come up with a half-baked concept and then frame it up with a weak acronym to try to pull the concept together. That said.... I couldn't resist.

B – (yeah, I couldn't think of anything to put here)
E – (yeah, here either)

Prepare Yourself – Mentally prepare to "tune in" and Be Present.
Remove the Distractions – Everything you can – sounds, people, devices, etc.
Engage Your Focus – Direct all of your focus, body language and responses to them.
See the Need – and fill it. What do they want from this interaction?
Enjoy the Time – This moment won't ever come again.
Nurture – this relationship. It is of worth to them and to you.
Thank Them – they won't expect it but will appreciate it.

Takeaways:

- Develop a plan to train yourself to be present.
- Practice the mental and physical habits.
- Use the right words, phrases and questions to connect.
- Small habits, repeated daily can be the secret to YOUR success.
- Use the acronym to create and maintain the habit.

Quote:

"Today is life-the only life you are sure of. Make the most of today. Get interested in something. Shake yourself awake. Develop a hobby. Let the winds of enthusiasm sweep through you. Live today with gusto."
-- Dale Carnegie

26 - MEDITATING SHMEDITATING

This is where I lose a lot of people when I try to tie meditating into **Being Present**. I even lose those who take the time to pray with no interruptions versus those who are blessed to be able to do it in lite traffic. Having said that, I literally hate (why yes it IS a strong word) those of you who do it while we are all waiting for the left turn arrow in traffic. You people are NOT going to the good place when you pass away!

There seems to be a negative stigma attached to meditating that I truly don't understand.

Three Myths:

1. You have to wear Tibetan Monk or Home Depot or UT Orange. I personally prefer the shade of orange found in the Gators jersey!
2. You have to be sitting in a pretzel coil and cramping.
3. You have to make that sound (mantra) that is similar to having a sonic care toothbrush in your mouth.

Jason Billows (jasonbillows.com and stopandbreath.com) is a cool guy and a great resource who was kind enough to allow me to include his "10 Step Beginner Guide to Meditation" below.

1. Sit Tall

The most common and accessible position for meditation is sitting. Sit on the floor, in a chair or on a stool. If you are seated on the floor it is often most comfortable to sit cross-legged on a cushion. Comfort is key. Now imagine a thread extending from the top of your head, pulling your back, neck and head straight up towards the ceiling in a straight line. Sit tall.

2. Relax your Body

Close your eyes and scan your body, relaxing each body part one at a time. Begin with your toes, feet, ankles, shins and continue to move up your entire body. Don't forget to relax your shoulders, neck, eyes, face, jaw and tongue which are all common areas for us to hold tension.

3. Be Still and Silent

Now that you are sitting tall and relaxed, take a moment to be still. Just sit. Be aware of your surroundings, your body, the sounds around you. Don't react or attempt to change anything. Just be aware.

4. Breathe

Turn your attention to your breath. Breathe silently, yet deeply. Engage your diaphragm and fill your lungs, but do not force your breath. Notice how your breath feels in your nose, throat, chest and belly as it flows in and out.

5. Establish a Mantra

A mantra is a sound, word or phrase that can be repeated throughout your meditation. Mantras can have spiritual, vibrational and transformative benefits, or they can simply provide a point of focus during meditation. They can be spoken aloud or silently to yourself. A simple and easy mantra for beginners is to silently say with each breath, *I am breathing in, I am breathing out.*

6. Calm Your Mind

As you focus on your breath or mantra, your mind will begin to calm and become present. This does not mean that thoughts will cease to arise. As thoughts come to you, simply acknowledge them, set them aside, and return your attention to your breath or mantra. Don't dwell on your thoughts. Some days your mind will be busy and filled with inner chatter, other days it will remain calm and focused. Neither is good, nor bad.

9. When to End Your Practice

There is no correct length of time to practice meditation, however when first beginning it is often easier to sit for shorter periods of time (5 to 10 minutes). As you become more comfortable with your practice, meditate longer. Set an alarm if you prefer to sit for a predetermined length of time. Another option is to decide on the number of breaths you will count before ending your practice. A **mala** is a helpful tool to use when counting breaths.

8. How to End Your Practice

When you are ready to end your practice, slowing bring your conscious attention back to your surroundings. Acknowledge your presence in the space around
you. Gently wiggle your fingers and toes. Begin to move your hands, feet, arms and legs. Open your eyes. Move slowly and take your time getting up.

9. Practice Often

Consistency is more important than quantity. Meditating for 5 minutes every day will reward you with far greater benefits than meditating for two hours, one day a week.

10. Practice Everywhere

Most beginners find it easier to meditate in a quiet space at home, but as you become more comfortable, begin exploring new places to practice. Meditating outdoors in nature can be very peaceful and taking the opportunity to meditate on the bus or in your office chair can be an excellent stress reliever.

Meditation is a simple, effective and convenient way to calm your busy mind, relax your body, become grounded and find inner peace amidst the chaos of day-to-day life. Begin meditating today and reap the rewards.

OK – so there are his 10 and they work! What's the worst that can happen if you give it a try? Cramps?

Meditating is the original trigger for self-awareness and *Being Present*! There may be nothing better for relieving stress.

And now the number of ways and reasons to meditate is equal to my daily calorie consumption. There are literally thousands. Once you get hooked, you won't stop.

Try it and you too could be a master-meditator (it's a word – look it up) in no time and benefit from the many reasons even more compelling than *Being Present*. Yes I just said that. (Note to self - consider striking from final book draft copy)

Do this – YOU deserve it and oh by the way, nobody can take THIS thing of value from you!

Takeaways:

- Meditating isn't difficult.
- The benefits are numerous, and you don't even have to go to the gym!
- It is the original way to be present!

Quote:

"When one door closes another door opens; but we so often look so long and so regretfully upon the closed door, that we do not see the ones which open for us." -- Alexander Graham Bell

27 - AFFIRMATIONS AND ICONOGRAPHY

Affirmations are a great way to support your personal efforts in **Being Present**. Affirmations are just an easy way to affect positive self-talk.

What you tell yourself is what you become.

Iconography is a simple medium that can support the same efforts to being present. They are visual images and symbols that are traditionally used in a work of art or the study of one. We can use them as visual anchors for your big brain!

Both of these are like having the effect of a tuning fork for your heart. It will help align you to what you say is important to you. They are reminders, one with words and one as a picture that when you look at it reminds you of what you have SAID is important to you. Once you see them you then have to reconcile whether you are "in tune" or on track with it or not. If you are, then you gain extra emotional strength to continue. If you are not, then it creates this internal emotional discord that you then recognize and then have to reconcile.

You can't continue to act in a way not in alignment with that you SAY is important and not create some personal strife. The end result is normally that you work harder next time to make sure you are acting in accordance and in a short period of time you ARE!

Affirmations

Can affirmations be aspirational versus 100% true in that moment? Absolutely and in fact that is part of why they are so good at affecting positive personal change. I include the affirmation process in anything I want to change about myself. Whether that is to start doing something good or stop doing something bad. There is nothing more powerful than positive self-talk.

What might an affirmation look like to help you? It is just writing down the things you want to hear yourself say to you, multiple times a day. Tape one on your bathroom mirror, keep a copy folded in your pocket, make it your screen saver, etc.

Here is sample one you could consider modifying to make it your own. Remember that the statement is not 100% true when you start the effort. It will feel uncomfortable at first but just keep plugging away at it and you will the difference very quickly.

BEING PRESENT AFFIRMATION

I am a master at **Being Present**.

I "begin with the end in mind" when I prepare to interact with someone.

I remove all mental and physical distractions and I declare myself ready to connect with them.

I use my posture, my facial expressions, my attentiveness to allow me to get and give the most to this interaction.

I always make the other person feel comfortable that I am 100% engaged with them. They know I am present in this moment and nowhere else.

I always position myself to remove and visual distractions.

I am an expert at discerning what the other person needs from this interaction. I am an incredible active listener and only interrupt when clarification is necessary.

They can tell by my level of engagement that our relationship is of value to me.

They always know that they have been heard.

I always thank them for making time for us and sharing with me.

Now if you read this 20 minutes before the interaction do you think you might act or react differently as a result of being exposed to the message? The answer is a big honk'in YES! Of course, you will.

You've just imprinted your intent at the front of your mind. You're about to doing something great and they are probably going to notice either in the moment or on the car drive home.

THIS WORKS!

Iconography

The definition of iconography is "the visual images and symbols used in a work of art or the study or interpretation of these".
What I take from that and apply here is the use of visuals to help myself and others mentally ANCHOR on specific words, phrases or concepts that represent what we want to focus on. These can be pictures, diagrams or anything else that visually helps keep you on track to your objective or even process. You may have recently seen examples of a variation on this theme called infographics. It takes the key components of a message or process and puts it into a communication that includes picture and word key points. It doesn't matter what you call it – IT WORKS!

A not good but GREAT example (yeah – I'm bragging) is a simple 3 x 5 pocket card that WILL make an immediate impact if used. Try it, go ahead – I dare ya.

Prepare Yourself
Remove the Distractions
Engage Your Focus
See the Need
Enjoy the Time
Nurture This Relationship
Thank Them

Another tool I know of other folks using is to simply write *Be Present* at the top of the piece of paper they are using whether in a personal or professional environment. I've heard that seeing that simple reminder has made all the difference for keeping them on track in the interaction. I'm told that even when it's not an interaction and they are just in a meeting and a supposed to be engaged it helps them do exactly that. One person has also told me that they write "BP" at the top of each page. They said that many times their page is visible and when someone sees *Be Present,* they ask why it is there and what it means, etc. They told me even though the person appreciates the explanation, it's a pain in the butt to explain every time so they just use the initials.

Takeaways:

- Affirmations help you become what you want to be. They don't have to be 100% true in this moment as they are aspirational. Read them or even a subset of them as many times as you can logistically manage a day. Some do it every hour, every other hour, at 9, 12, 3 and 6:00. Some read in their driveway to ground them in the same behavior before they walk in the door at home.
- Iconography is a cool visual reminder that anchors something important in your big brain. Figure out how to put the important messages that keep you inside the guardrails you want in front of you. Notecards or screen savers are great ways to keep the message up front in your head!

Quote:

"It is a mistake to look too far ahead. The chain of destiny can only be grasped one link at a time."
- - Sir Winston Churchill

28 - PEOPLE WILL NOTICE

If you begin to use the concepts described here to be present, the reactions you will soon get will be very interesting and I hope very impactful to you.

Most people aren't used to receiving the level of engagement associated with someone actually *Being Present*. You will likely see a wide array of reactions. I've had people tell me it scared the $h!snit (proverbial poop) out of them. They were so used to the surface level interactions that something more engaging was so unfamiliar that it made them very uncomfortable. My favorite story was "The eye contact was so intense I was sure you were either trying to hypnotize me or distract me so you could pick my pocket." It can be perceived as intense and in some cases unnerving.

The interesting thing about people noticing that you are *Being Present* is that almost everyone notices... eventually. The exception is that one completely self- absorbed person. You know the one. Mentally fill in their name here. They may not notice consciously but what they do appreciate is that they feel good about the interaction.

For everyone else you hear them notice it early in the interactions and sometimes it takes a while.

Sometimes you hear it at the end of a conversation when they tell you "OMG – I didn't even let you get a word in. I'm so sorry but you are so easy to talk to. I feel like you get me." (You did it!)

When their defenses come down it's "OMG – I can't even believe I told you that. You just seem so open and non-judgy." (landed a 10!)

Or when your daughter who is like one of my daughters it's – "OMG chatting was so like, I mean like, really really like nice. If you want like want another like Starbucks, I'm totally like down with that. I mean like, totes." (I'm NOT EVEN kidding.)

"Hey – I truly appreciate you listening to me." (You have arrived at your Being Present destination!)

How will you respond when you hear one or most of these? I have no idea what you will say but I DO KNOW how you will feel. All warm, brown and runny inside!

What will eventually hook you and make you want to be even better at *Being Present* is the sense of satisfaction in knowing you are honoring a behavior that is of tremendous value to OTHERS. Not to you – but to them. Sure, you will feel better about doing it, but you will feel GREAT seeing the impact on others. Then you will get hooked and even more people will notice. It has even been known to make people's eye's leak with joy.

Eventually some of those people will connect the mental dots and also want to be better at **being present**. They will engage and ask you about it. And won't that be a great present for you?

Takeaways:

• Be prepared – people will notice. Decide how you will respond. What will your story be about why doing this is important to you?

• When you notice that they notice, you will be hooked for life! What an incredible present, being present is to yourself!

Quote:

"You must live in the present, launch yourself on every wave, find your eternity in each moment. Fools stand on their island opportunities and look toward another land. There is no other land, there is no other life but this."
-- Henry David Thoreau

29 - SUMMARY

The name of this book is **Being Present** and subtitled "A Guide to Connecting". The truth is that the objective of this book is to "connect" and **Being Present** is simply the best way to do that.

When you consider connecting better with those you care about or even having richer engagements with anyone, think about the reason WHY. Why at your core do you want to connect better? I would submit it is because you WANT to be better and that you recognize that you CAN be.

A few times the habits I've described and associated with **Being Present** have been perceived as manipulative tactics and nothing could be further from the truth. Creating those good habits because you want to do the right thing makes all the difference in the world. If your "spirit of intent" is in the right place, then you should feel good about creating those better habits and using the learnings here to help you do that.

I mentioned before that I fail every day and it's still so true. Also true is that I am better in ALL areas of my life for the focus I've given this subject. What has come with it is a clarity and enrichment in my life that is most times difficult to describe.

So, what do you do now? I believe the answer is relatively simple and formulaic – though I have to also say that I'm not always 100% present and you'd probably guess that if I thought I could author this book I'd at least be pretty good at it. Truth is that I am pretty good at it but it's a journey and the best I can tell you is that you will reach a point where you are OK with where you've ended up. Meaning that you know and can see and have probably been told that you are better. I think any of us would start in the process with differing entry points and different needs to get out of it. Hey – if you're reading this book and it's a "voluntary read" – you've already started!

AND since you've ended up reading these final pages then I know something about you EVEN MORE than you know about you. You ALREADY see value in *Being Present* for yourself and those you care about. The stories and messages resonated with you. You saw and heard yourself in those pages. You WILL do something with the information you've been exposed to. You will try to and be SUCCESSFUL at this. You will be better!

And THAT's why I wanted to share this concept. My "why" for this effort is very simple. I take a tremendous amount of gratification from helping others. Maybe it was too many Sunday School classes when I was young or just having good parents, but it does drive me. It is my "why" and I hope this helps you or someone else you care about.

Good Luck!

Final Quote:

*"The greatest gift you can give another person is **being present**."*

-- Casey K. McEwen

Casey K. McEwen

ABOUT THE AUTHOR

Casey is a tall, semi-handsome modest married man with four awesome kids
and lives in Atlanta, Georgia.
His talents are marginal, but he has a fantastic sense of humor.

Made in the USA
Columbia, SC
20 April 2021